NIGHT THOUGHTS

❖❖❖

Martin Israel

SPCK

First published in Great Britain 1990

SPCK
Holy Trinity Church
Marylebone Road
London NW1 4DU

Acknowledgements

Biblical quotations from the New English Bible © 1970 are
reproduced by permission of Oxford and Cambridge
University Presses.

The extract from 'Burnt Norton' from *Four Quartets* from
Collected Poems 1909–1962 by T. S. Eliot is reproduced
by permission of Faber and Faber Ltd and Harcourt Brace
Jovanovich Inc, Orlando, Florida.

British Library Cataloguing in Publication Data

Israel, M. S. (Martin Spencer),
    Night thoughts.
    1. Quotations.   For Christianity.
    I. Title
    208.88'2

    ISBN 0-281-04448-1

Typeset by Pioneer Associates (Graphic) Ltd
Printed in Great Britain by
Biddles Ltd, Guildford and King's Lynn

Contents

Preface

❖❖

This group of meditations is designed for reading towards the end of the day, when the various events have had time to make their impression and given us cause to reflect more deeply on the course of our life as mirrored in the microcosm of the passing scene. They are not designed merely to soothe and send to sleep, valuable as this function is. They are also here to' challenge us about the truth which underlies our attitudes and actions. When we proceed fearlessly about this business of clear confrontation we find, much to our relief, that the way is radiantly expectant, firmly based on the love of God for his creatures and his patient striving for their resurrection to eternal life. This is the perfection which Jesus demands of us; a perfection of love that cares for everything around us so that finally all is brought back to the Creator intact and entire.

It is when we are in this frame of mind that sleep is not only a welcome period of oblivion from the troubles that encompass us, but also a time of renewal when we shall awake refreshed and heartened, ready to carry on what life has in store for us the next day.

Martin Israel
July 1989

Bless the Lord, my soul;
  my innermost heart, bless his holy name.
Bless the Lord, my soul,
  and forget none of his benefits.

Psalm 103.1—2

Almighty God,
by whose grace we are sustained day by day,
grant that we may serve thy church in continuous prayer
and thy people in unfailing service,
through Jesus Christ, our Lord,
who lives and reigns
with thee and the Holy Spirit,
now and for ever.

Prayer for Holy Trinity Church,
Martin Israel

ONE

God's Presence Among Us

The Kingdom of God

> 'Tis ye, 'tis your estrangèd faces,
> That miss the many-splendoured thing.

Francis Thompson, 'The Kingdom of God'

It is recorded in Luke 17.20–21, that when the Pharisees asked Jesus when the kingdom of God would come, he replied that one cannot tell its advent by observation, so as to point directly to it. In fact the kingdom of God is within, or among, us all now. The choice of prepositions offers alternate sides of the same coin, for the kingdom is both a part of our spiritual essence and a state of communal, eventually world-wide, harmony among the various forces of humanity that are usually in destructive conflict. In his day Jesus could mediate that kingdom to all who would receive him. Thus he instructed the twelve disciples to proclaim the message, 'The kingdom of Heaven is upon you', when he sent them forth on their preliminary missionary journey. A proof of the reality of this kingdom was to be their healing work among the sick, the lepers, the dead and those infested by evil spirits (Matt. 10.7–8).

Heaven is a state of inner wholeness. When one is in heaven, one is completely and unashamedly oneself, open to the glory of the world around one, and as transparent in one's simplicity as others are transparent in their innate goodness. There is a spark of nobility in even the most degraded person, and when we know the heavenly light, we evoke the best from all those around us. So it was with the heavenly man Jesus: when people were with him they no longer needed to justify themselves, for there was no longer any judgement against them. The love of God flowed through him to them, and they were suddenly liberated from their past restrictions that prevented them from being open to the world in the present moment.

It is, however, a hard thing to bear the full power of love. Love divests us of all previous illusions of importance, power and prestige. It cuts us down to size in order to raise us up to the divine image in which we were orginally created. This is a state of being

2

in which we may know God in mystical union, and work towards the coming of his kingdom by the full use of our body, mind and soul. Ceasing to be powerful in our own right, we become the vehicles of the divine power.

> And we are put on earth a little space,
> that we may learn to bear the beams of love.

So wrote William Blake in 'The Little Black Boy'.

It must be said in all honesty that not everyone responds to God's love in this way; free will remains inviolate, and we can reject that love as the religious leaders of Christ's day rejected the love that he beamed on the world. Why did they reject Christ's love? Because they were self-sufficient and could not tolerate the suggestion that they needed the help of anyone else. Furthermore, in the face of heaven we see ourselves very clearly. This is why it is so hard to bear the beams of love: our pride responds by inflating itself to unseemly proportions, and until it is deflated by a fall, it will exclude any assistance from outside. The very pious type of individual is sometimes so bewitched by his or her own impeccable rectitude that any suggestion of fallibility is a dire threat to the self-imposed image, which the person will fight to the death to preserve. And so it may come about that a traditional religious type of heaven imprisons its devotees in hell, whereas the penitent sinner that we all are in our better moments is firmly at home in a heaven that excludes nobody except by the person's own choice. 'Thou wast with me, and I was not with thee', wrote St Augustine in his *Confessions*. Indeed, God is always with us, and when we are quiet at the end of a day's busy, and often frustrating, work the divine presence is at last allowed to beam love into our tired souls.

I thank you, Lord, for your unceasing presence in your creation. May I attain that quiet attention to the present moment by which to know you and to serve you best.

3

God With Us

❖❖❖❖❖❖❖❖❖❖❖❖❖❖❖❖❖❖❖❖❖❖ ❖❖❖❖❖❖❖❖❖❖❖❖❖❖❖❖❖❖❖❖❖❖❖❖❖❖❖

> I will be with you, and I will protect you wherever you go and
> will bring you back to this land; for I will not leave you until I
> have done all that I have promised.
>
> Genesis 28.15

This promise of God's help and protection spurred the rather crafty
Jacob on his way to Mesopotamia where he fled to escape the wrath
of his twin Esau whom he had tricked. He was to dwell with his
even shiftier kinsman Laban and marry Laban's two daughters
Leah and Rachel before he could stand his uncle's dishonesty no
longer. Then he fled once more, this time back to Canaan where he
had to face his now powerful chieftain brother Esau, who could
easily have destroyed Jacob and his small retinue. Instead, Jacob
found himself engaged in combat with the angel of the Lord, an
amazing and obscure encounter which left him permanently
crippled but with the moral stature of a patriarch. He was now
indeed Israel, one who had contended with God and survived to
become his champion.

I believe we all have a special part to play in the world during our
brief sojourn here. While some people are obviously gifted and
marked out, at least potentially, for higher things, most of us live
outwardly undistinguished lives, just getting on with the business
at hand. It is how we get on with our work that matters, rather
than its distinction in the world's eyes. It is far better to be a good
husband and father, mother and housewife, than to shine in the
world of science, politics or religion yet create havoc in one's
personal relationships. 'In the days before the flood they ate and
drank and married, until the day that Noah went into the ark, and
they knew nothing until the flood came and swept them all away'
(Matt. 24.38–39). Here was a population living thoughtlessly,
totally unworthy of inhabiting the earth; and so they were swept
from its surface. This situation was to be repeated in a historical
setting when the inhabitants of the northern kingdom of Israel
(Samaria) were swallowed up by the Assyrian army, and those of
Judah by the Babylonians.

Just as God made a covenant with the Israelites, so he makes one with each of us; but we have to play our part. The tragic story of the Old Testament is of the continual abrogation of that covenant on the part of the people: they separate themselves from God and the life-giving power of his Spirit. There is no life in them until they repent. But once we keep our vows of constancy, God does not leave us.

To be sure, we are poor stuff: the spirit is willing, but the flesh is weak, as Jesus observed of Peter, James and John in the Gethsemane episode (Matt. 26.41); but we are also 'such stuff as dreams are made on', as Shakespeare says in *The Tempest*. If we pray continually, as St Paul exhorts in 1 Thessalonians 5.16–18, we can always know an inner joy even when circumstances are bad, and we will learn quite spontaneously to give thanks whatever happens. We will begin to see, when we are in close fellowship with God in prayer, how adversity strengthens the flesh and how the dream that is the pinnacle of every life, no matter how undistinguished that life may appear in worldly eyes, may slowly attain actualization. God did not make Jacob's life easy, any more than he mollified the terrible sufferings of his chosen prophet Jeremiah. But both of them attained the full stature of a real person, and their contribution to the spiritual development of the human race has been incalculable.

So let us also, when we rub our aching bones and seek to soothe our fevered emotions after a particularly harrowing period in our lives, call with confidence on the name of God in prayer that does not falter in constancy and faith. 'Be assured,' says Jesus, 'I am with you always, to the end of time' (Matt. 28.20).

I thank you, Lord, for your unfailing presence in my life. Make me so obedient to the high calling ahead of me that I never stray from you in the heated outburst of the passing moment.

Trust in God

❖❖❖❖❖❖❖❖❖❖❖❖❖❖❖❖❖❖❖❖❖ ❖❖❖❖❖❖❖❖❖❖❖❖❖❖❖❖❖❖❖❖❖❖❖❖

Come back, keep peace, and you will be safe;
in stillness and in staying quiet, there lies your strength.

Isaiah 30.15

This text refers to the desperate attempt of the government of Judah under its enlightened, beneficent king Hezekiah, to muster support from the pharaoh of Egypt against the invading Assyrian army, which pillaged indiscriminately wherever it entered. Indeed, the people of the northern kingdom of Israel disappeared for ever under the horror of Assyrian deportation, and it seemed only too probable that the inhabitants of Judah would fare likewise, while the sacred city of Jerusalem and the Temple would be razed to the ground. If only the people could have trusted in the Lord, all would have been well. In the event the besieging Assyrian host suddenly departed from Jerusalem, for reasons which remain obscure, and the city was miraculously saved. And so Isaiah's oracle was fulfilled, despite rather than because of Hezekiah's activities.

When the burden of difficulties is almost too great for us to bear, when we are the victims of a tragedy of enormous proportion, a deeper wisdom will eventually guide our response and modify our actions. We remember Hamlet's soliloquy:

To be, or not to be: that is the question:
Whether 'tis nobler in the mind to suffer
The slings and arrows of outrageous fortune,
Or to take arms against a sea of troubles,
And by opposing end them?

It seems that both these options have their point, but the wise person will have learned by life's experience that patient suffering is the best preparation for positive action against misfortune, such as is bound to cloud all lives that are moving towards the ultimate meaning. It was this meaning that Hamlet himself was seeking; the spiritual aspirant knows that the great work is himself or herself. The place of operation is where we find ourselves, and our tools are the means at hand. It is hard to attain this stance of cool detachment when our little world seems to be going up in smoke,

6

but we maintain our greatest calm when we trust in the providence of God, admitting that of ourselves we can do nothing to alter the situation.

> Let be then: learn that I am God,
> high over the nations, high above earth. (Psalm 46.10)

The psalmist here reminds us that God is our shelter and our refuge, a timely help in trouble. Therefore neither the tumult of the cosmic elements nor the destructive fury of invading armies need fill us with terror.

These things are bound to be, as part of the evolution of the universe and our own growth into full humanity. Their pain cannot be denied, but the end is so vast in its human implications that we may be able to say with Job:

> I know that thou canst do all things
> and that no purpose is beyond thee.
> But I have spoken of great things which I have not understood,
> things too wonderful for me to know.
> I knew thee then only by report,
> but now I see thee with my own eyes.
> Therefore I melt away;
> I repent in dust and ashes. (Job 42.2-6)

A final point must be made: God does not do our work for us, nor does he rake our chestnuts out of the fire we have made. If he did, we would never grow into responsible people. The miraculous preservation of Jerusalem which we have considered did not profoundly alter the unspiritual attitude of the people, and little over a century later the city and its Temple were destroyed by the Babylonians. Only then did the remnant of the people think seriously of their covenant with God, and authentic Judaism was born under the teaching work of Ezra and his successors. God's action is one of strengthening us, so that we may be better equipped to deal with the emergency.

Give me the faith to be still when danger threatens, Lord, so that I may be receptive to the power of your Spirit and acquit myself as an authentic person modelled on your nature as revealed in Jesus Christ.

The Divine Indwelling

I saw God in a point, that is to say, in mine understanding — by which sight I saw that he is in all things.

Julian of Norwich, *Revelations of Divine Love*, ch. 11

Mother Julian, in company with many of the world's greatest mystics, saw true: there is nothing too small to be without him, for by him all things come to be. And yet, by his infinite courtesy, the attribute of God stressed so often by Julian, he does not invade the privacy of his creatures nor forcibly determine their actions. The remarkable randomness of creation shows us how much the process is governed by sheer chance and by the self-governing principles within each creature. But whereas in the lower orders of life chance is as likely to be harmful as beneficial, in the case of us humans everything can ultimately turn out for good, provided we have the staying power to persist despite all discouragement. St Paul's belief that all things work together for good for those who love God (Rom. 8.28) is vindicated time after time when we have the faith to proceed in the darkness. The spiritual aspirant, when looking back on the course of his or her life, sees ever more clearly that nothing was fortuitous, but that everything worked towards increasing proficiency in all aspects of existence. The hard times are there for our strengthening, while the times of plenty allow us to enjoy the fruits of our labour as well as God's greater bounty to all his creatures.

Though the Creator has left his creation free to get on with its own business, the process of evolution in all its intricacies, he has left a spark of himself with us to guide us on our way. But we do not have to follow the light; we can as easily go our own way regardless of the guidance offered, like Adam and Eve or the builders of the Tower of Babel, to say nothing of the repeated apostasies of the children of Israel throughout the entire Old Testament period. This is the nature of sin, which, as Julian was shown, also has its inscrutable part to play in bringing us nearer our Creator. 'Thou hast made us for thyself, and the heart of man is restless until it finds its rest in thee', writes St Augustine at the

8

beginning of his *Confessions*; later he regrets, 'Thou wast with me, and I was not with thee'. Sin, by humiliating us when its fruits become apparent, clears away the assertiveness of the ego, and makes us more aware of what is going on in our depths. Then we are open to listen intently and hear intelligently what the Holy Spirit within us is telling us.

Julian writes, in chapter 53 of her book: 'In every soul that shall be saved is a godly will that never assented to sin, nor ever shall.' To amplify this enormous statement, repeated often by the mystics, especially by Meister Eckhart, we see in 1 Timothy 2.4, that it is God's will that all humans should find salvation and come to know the truth. Therefore the 'godly will' is present in the apex of the soul, called the spirit, of all of us. But we have to respond to it. Whereas the humbler forms of life proceed unconsciously on their evolutionary path, the human is able to co-operate with the divine will and lift up the whole creation to a new height of excellence. But there is also the potentiality for terrible destruction if self-will prevails. The closer we follow to the divine spark, the more we are motivated by love. In Julian's revelation, recorded in chapter 5 of her book, she saw the whole creation symbolized as a mere hazel nut in the palm of her hand. She marvelled that it did not immediately disintegrate because of its smallness, but was told that it was eternally preserved because God loved it. 'And so all-thing hath the being by the love of God. In this little thing I saw three properties. The first is that God made it, the second is that God loveth it, the third, that God keepeth it.'

May I always remember your providence, Lord, when all is disorder around me and all is turmoil within me. May I remember then especially to lift up my mind to you in prayer, for then alone can I work for your greater design in creation.

❖❖❖❖❖❖
TWO
❖❖❖❖❖❖

Shafts of Light on the Path of Knowing Ourselves

Mixed Motives and
their Acceptance

❖❖❖❖❖❖❖❖❖❖❖❖❖❖❖❖❖❖❖❖ ❖❖❖❖❖❖❖❖❖❖❖❖❖❖❖❖❖❖❖❖❖❖❖❖❖❖❖❖❖❖❖❖❖❖

Once, when I was thinking how it distressed me to eat meat and
do no penance, I heard the words, 'Sometimes there is more
self-love in such a thought than desire for penance.'

St Teresa of Avila, *Spiritual Relations*, 65

The context of this thought was an illness of St Teresa at Toledo in
1576–7, when her confessor restricted her penances and ordered
her to eat meat. Our motives are indeed mixed. How often do we
believe we have another person's welfare at heart, when in truth
we need the exercise of power to dominate others! When our own
sense of inner security is uneasy, it is a relief to escape from the
perilous situation within and start to meddle in affairs that are not
our business.

But is another's welfare never our business? Jesus teaches us
that our neighbour is the person close at hand. And we, like the
Good Samaritan, must always be aware of our neighbour so as to
offer assistance should the occasion arise. However, before we can
be properly aware of another's difficulty, we first have to get our
own perception in order. In practice the two proceed together. As
we attain some degree of inner health, so we are able to assist our
neighbour more effectively. The relationship, in turn, strengthens
our own power of endurance and sharpens our awareness so that
we become more conscious of our own deficiencies. These we can
lift up to God in prayer for healing, so that we can serve better.

As St Teresa noted, religious duties can easily become focuses of
self-adulation. This applies also to self-denial, where there may be
an additional factor of masochism, a psychological aberration in
which the person derives pleasure (especially sexual) from pain or
humiliation. Our haloes can shine particularly brightly when we
believe we are suffering pain for Christ's sake. How easily we use
him for our own self-satisfaction while deluding ourselves that we
really love him! We should be especially wary when we feel a glow

12

of spiritual satisfaction. The test is that of the Pharisee in the famous parable of Luke 18.9–14: do we look down on others from our pinnacle of spiritual advancement? If so, we are truly the least of all our fellows.

How then are we to approach the mixed motives that seem to cloud so many of our endeavours? In fact, the method is quite simple: do the obviously noble thing, but with your eyes open. Give glory to God as the results show themselves, and let him sort out the tangle of emotions that lie near the heart of your works. It is better to succour and provide for the traveller on the road from Jerusalem to Jericho (which is a paradigm of our earthly journey) who has been assailed by criminals, than to leave the person to the mercy of the inclement elements of the weather, even if there is a surreptitious hope for general acclaim when our action is made public. As we continue to act in a spirit of charity, so we shall find ourselves thinking less about our own image; entering into the pain of a fellow creature will increasingly release us from the enclosure of self. Our heart becomes more open to God's love and our personality is renewed. We begin to see that the entire life of an aspiring person is a penance for the inconsideration of the past.

The real suffering comes as one realizes that one has missed the mark; the cure is a free confession of the trouble to God, and the privilege is to be used to help one's neighbour in distress. This is the service of perfect freedom, for now one is no longer attached to rewards of any kind, either in this world or the next. Virtue is its own reward; to do good, by which I mean to further God's reign of love in the world, is the finest action we can conceive.

Bring me, Lord, to a constant awareness of my own weaknesses, so that by your unfailing love I may be able to accept myself in the round. When I have known your unconditional acceptance, may I be able to accept the frailties of other people and love them for themselves alone.

The Candid Admission
of Error

❖❖❖❖❖❖❖❖❖❖❖❖❖❖❖❖❖❖❖❖❖ ❖❖❖❖❖❖❖❖❖❖❖❖❖❖❖❖❖❖❖❖❖❖❖❖❖❖❖

Never be ashamed to admit your mistakes.

Ecclesiasticus 4.26

It is hard to admit our errors, because a front of infallibility hides
the quaking inadequacy underneath; indeed, we depend very heavily
on the affirmation of those whose opinions we especially value. A
dark look from them, or even a peep askance, may shatter, at least
temporarily, our self-confidence. It is a painful lesson to stand on
our own unsteady feet.

It must be very satisfying to be always right, for then everyone
else can look up to one as to a minor god; but such an individual, if
he or she really existed, would in the end be an object of pity rather
than adulation! Life is growth, and the person who has attained
absolute mastery so as to be the authority in all matters is closer to
death than most of us would reckon. In fact, the real masters of
particular disciplines are always aware of their deficiencies, and so
are not only open to new insights but actually welcome them.

If this is true of scientific work, it is even more true of the
spiritual life. The spiritual aspirant (to be sharply contrasted with
the seeker after esoteric knowledge, who is driven by an ego lusting
for power) is never far from his or her unconscious roots.
Awareness of unworthiness is never far from the surface, and this
produces a true humility. Far from rejecting outside criticism, it is
accepted, painful as it so often is, with gratitude, and acted upon
with diligence. As St Paul reminds us, 'All alike have sinned, and
are deprived of the divine splendour' (Rom. 3.23). The greatest
saints have confessed their unworthiness, but God, while affirming
their assessment of their inner lives, has reminded them that he is
worthy. We are justified, brought into right relationship with God,
by faith, which means a childlike trust, and not by any works that
we may do. These works interpose the self-seeking ego between
God and us, so spoiling the relationship and ultimately ruining the

works themselves. On the other hand, when we are in right relationship with God, love informs our efforts, which then become a blessing to many.

It is interesting that the expression 'to lose face', which means to be humiliated, to lose one's credit or good name, is of Chinese origin (according to the Oxford Dictionary it is a translation of *tiu lien*). In the Far East losing face is especially detestable, a fact of interest since the dominant religious systems stress the illusion of the ego, which is the power behind the face. In the Christian mode, the love of a personal God (manifested in the sacrifice of Christ for the sins of the whole world) can embrace the wounded face with forgiveness, so that it emerges more beautiful than ever before; its wounds have become worships, as Mother Julian of Norwich would put it. And so the sinful ego can be redeemed into loving service for God, the most glorious of all freedoms.

The quotation from Ecclesiasticus above ends with the injunction, 'nor try to swim against the current'. Our mistakes will always find us out in the end, and attempts to conceal them from God are as fruitless as trying to swim against a river's flow. Furthermore, our fellow humans will find us out very quickly too; like the emperor in Hans Andersen's story, our nakedness will be apparent to all except ourselves, eventually to be exposed by a small child. Therefore be kind to yourself, especially as the day closes and the night draws in for the period of sleep. But first make an inventory of the mistakes you have made, and then give them to God as your sacrifice on the altar of your heart. He will relieve you of them, so that you can go to bed disembarrassed of the guilt and misgivings which so rob one of sleep. Provided we have had the integrity to face our errors, the humility to give them to God, and the intention to be more careful in future, we may rest quietly, as the period of repose prepares us for the tasks of the next day.

May I have the courage and honesty to face my mistakes squarely and without equivocation, Lord, so that my humiliation may be the source of compassion and healing to others.

The Power of the Tongue

✦✦✦✦✦✦✦✦✦✦✦✦✦✦✦✦✦✦✦✦✦ ✦✦✦✦✦✦✦✦✦✦✦✦✦✦✦✦✦✦✦✦✦✦✦✦✦

Never remain silent when a word might put things right.

Ecclesiasticus 4.23

How enclosed our lives are as we pursue the daily round in heedless haste, so often oblivious of the thoughts and feelings of those around us! If we are conscientious in our work, we may find the apparent carelessness of our fellows increasingly irksome until at last our irritation breaks forth in words and gestures of impatience and exasperation. In themselves these are not to be denied; bottling up our emotions under the guise of gentility or virtue with a subtle undercurrent of martyrdom does our health no good, while our relationship with the person who disturbs our equilibrium founders inwardly even if we assume a mask of tolerant graciousness. The truth will come out in the end, in the process freeing us from the barely tolerable tension of restraint, but at the same time burdening us with a sense of regret as we feel that we have failed the test of compassion and have allowed our selfish attitude to triumph over a concern for the other person.

> What an immense stack of timber can be set ablaze by the tiniest spark! And the tongue is in effect a fire. It represents among our members the world with all its wickedness; it pollutes the whole being; it keeps the wheel of our existence red-hot, and its flames are fed by hell. Beasts and birds of every kind, creatures that crawl on the ground or swim in the sea, can be subdued and have been subdued by mankind; but no man can subdue the tongue. (Jas. 3.5–8)

Even apart from the deliberate malice suggested by this telling passage, the tongue is liable to spread gossip abroad by the simple thoughtlessness that is too much part of our daily relationships. And then there is the uncontrollable irritation which we have already considered. Speech may be silver, but silence is golden. If only we could learn to cultivate the practice of silence in daily life when verbal communication was unnecessary, we would be able to reflect before we spoke! Then the tongue would be under proper control, so that its subsequent utterances would be pertinent and helpful in fostering peace and goodwill.

But once the fateful word has escaped our lips, and at the end of the day we have the painful opportunity of recalling the possible havoc it has caused in our friendship with colleagues and neighbours, there comes a time for deeper reflection. What have I said, perhaps on the spur of the moment, that is hurting someone whose well-being I truly have at heart? So long as I stand on my pride and refuse to extend a hand of reconciliation, the hurt gnaws ever more deeply into my own soul, as I can imagine it doing likewise to the other person. And so a rift widens between us and the sullen face of enmity blurs our previous collaboration. At this juncture it is speech that is golden, and I must humble myself to put right what is gnawing at my conscience. This does not mean so much an abject apology, which may, indeed, be quite often ill-conceived if not hypocritical, but an honest attempt to sort out the difficulty, so that an authentic concern may embrace both of us in a new relationship of trust. 'Let us speak the truth in love' (Eph. 4.15). If the other person cannot accept that truth, the relationship will be effectively severed, at least until such time as a change of heart occurs. However, a relationship that cannot face the vicissitudes of human nature is *ipso facto* flimsy to the point of contrivance.

Give me, Lord, the courtesy to listen before I speak, the courage to hear the still small voice within, and the humility to confront my own unpleasantness in personal relationships. May I need no prompting to put right whatever my tongue may have uttered in unthinking haste or emotional stress.

Mary and Martha

❖❖❖❖❖❖❖❖❖❖❖❖❖❖❖❖❖❖❖❖ ❖❖❖❖❖❖❖❖❖❖❖❖❖❖❖❖❖❖❖❖❖❖❖❖❖

> If Martha had been like the Magdalene, rapt in contemplation,
> there would have been no one to give to eat to this divine Guest.

St Teresa of Avila, *The Way of Perfection*

The relative claims of action and contemplation may sometimes
come before us for consideration as the night draws on, and we
have a space to think about our day's work and our relationships
with those around us. The criterion of the day's success is measured
in the first case by the fruits of our labours, because these are
tangible and therefore available for calm assessment. On the surface
we may seem to have achieved what we set out to do, so that a
feeling of smug satisfaction may come over us. But then we come
to ponder more deeply on the people we have met and how we have
behaved towards them, especially our colleagues whom we know
very well through constant involvement. In the end it is
relationships that matter most, for the fruits of these last long after
the results of our material labours fade from view.

In the story of Mary (who probably, *pace* St Teresa, was not the
same person as Mary of Magdala) and Martha, Jesus visits their
home, and while Mary sits at his feet and listens to him, Martha is
left to prepare the meal. She becomes increasingly irritated that
she is left alone to do the work while her sister does nothing but
enjoy the presence of the Master. And so she tells Jesus to send
Mary out to help her; but the only reply she gets is a simple, kindly
but pointed, rebuke to the effect that she merely frets and fusses
about so many things, while her sister, in quiet contemplation, has
chosen the better way, and it will not be taken from her (Luke
10.38–42). From this rebuke has come the misunderstanding that
Jesus prizes contemplative inaction above work in the world. In
fact, it was Martha's attitude that he was censuring, not her work
in the kitchen. Her irritation was not occasioned by the simple
work she had to do, within the easy compass of a single individual,
but by the envy she felt at being excluded from the Master's
presence. Had her mind been concentrated on the work of preparing

18

the meal to the exclusion of all else, she would have been as close to God in contemplation as her sister. Instead of this priceless gift, she wanted acknowledgement and praise from Jesus.

It is obvious that, unless we play our part in the running of the world, all of us will quickly fade away as the earth fails to nourish us and also our animal brethren. Therefore the Martha function is immediately vindicated. But unless we are centred on a power greater than ourselves, we, like the builders of the Tower of Babel, will soon come to grief as personality problems thwart our labours and destroy our peace of mind. We remember Psalm 127.1–2: unless God builds the house or keeps watch over a city, all our human efforts are vain. Thus it comes about that contemplation should both precede and accompany action in the world. We finally come to realize that contemplation is the highest form of action; it is the willed ascent of the mind to God, who then fills us with the Holy Spirit, the one absolutely reliable guide to constructive action in the world.

And so we can understand Jesus' priority for the way of Mary. He would say to us, then, 'Go and do as she did', as in his advice to the lawyer whose query about the identity of one's neighbour evoked the parable of the Good Samaritan (Luke 10.37). St Teresa also makes the comment elsewhere that, 'to give our Lord a perfect hospitality, Mary and Martha must combine.' Ideally the two should combine in all of us as we sit in contemplation at the Lord's feet before we set out to do our chosen work in the world.

Lord, give me the courtesy to wait upon you in prayer before I proceed upon the many works that so fill me with pleasurable ambition, so that I may be aware of other people's welfare and seek to preserve it before my own desires.

A Matter of Priorities

Set your mind on God's kingdom and his justice before
everything else, and all the rest will come to you as well.

Matthew 6.33

This saying comes nearly at the end of Jesus' teaching on
detachment that forms an important part of the Sermon on the
Mount. He tells his audience not to be anxious about food and
clothes, since God takes care of the birds and the flowers. He
reminds them that all the worry in the world cannot add to their
growth. If the Almighty provides for the lower animals as well as
the plant kingdom, how much more he will care for them! The
human, by virtue of the rational mind and therefore the creative
potentiality given to him or her, is of greater value to God than any
of the non-rational creatures. These live on an instinctive level and
do not appear to be impelled by a purpose in life higher than
survival and procreation. The current interest in conservation has
indeed thrown light on the importance of animals and plants in the
maintenance of efficient ecosystems, but the creatures themselves
seem blissfully unaware of the contribution which their mere
presence makes to the stabilization of the environment.

And so, while God can feed the birds of the air with profligate
abandon, and attend to the needs of the humblest flower, we too
are upheld by his care and generosity. Without his constant presence
our lives would come to a severe halt, as would the life of our
planet and indeed the whole universe. Nevertheless, there is an
obvious difference between us and even our nearest primate
relatives: while they can depend entirely on God's care, we have to
play our full part. This is the responsibility that accrues from the
mental brilliance of the human and the free will associated with it.
The lilies of the field may be more splendidly attired than King
Solomon in all his regalia, but we will remain naked if we do not
exert ourselves to acquire clothes. Likewise we will starve to death
if we remain as passively dependent as the animals around us.
Human nature has its price.

Psalm 127.1–2 reminds us of the essential part which God plays in the conduct of such material affairs as building a house or keeping guard over a city; but nevertheless it is we who have to do the work, whether planning, toiling, or keeping watch. If we fall asleep, God will not annul the consequences of our negligence or folly. And so, therefore, how can we humans rely on God's providence when so much responsibility devolves upon us? Can we truly stop being anxious about the future economic situation of our country, upon which the common welfare depends?

The answer is given in Jesus' teaching: give your first priority to God, both in the practice of constant prayer and in the pursuit of the domestic and public virtues. These include honesty, sobriety, chastity and simplicity of life-style; they attain their fulfilment in the care of our neighbour that is the foundation of all civilized existence. When our mind is centred on these essential requirements for the good life, we will find that our natural faculties are much sharpened, and more efficient than before. There will be a close alignment of emotions and reason under the directing influence of our intuition, which in turn is closely inspired by the Holy Spirit. Whereas 'normally' we squander our psychic (and often physical) energy in emotional turmoil, when we are at one with ourselves under the divine direction our natural powers and gifts are used coherently; so that we can fend far more efficiently for ourselves and work more concertedly for the benefit of those close to us as well as of society generally. And so, indeed, we do not have to worry overmuch about our material situation, because we are able to cope with its demands as a matter of course, now that we are functioning as integrated people. As we serve God in constant awareness, so he fills us increasingly with the good things of life.

Teach me, Lord, so to remember you at every moment of my life that everything I do bears the impress of your love, even when I am so pressed for time that expediency seems the easiest way out of my difficulty. May your light then illuminate my mind, and your love inflame my heart to do what is required of me.

The Cardinal Sin of Pride

Unless the Lord builds the house,
its builders will have toiled in vain.

Psalm 127.1

The Psalmist goes on to state that unless the Lord keeps watch over a city, the watchman stands on guard in vain. The explanation of these assertions can best be found in an earlier portion of Scripture, the story of the Tower of Babel (Gen. 11.1–9). The people, full of hubris (insolent pride), decide to build a city for themselves and a tower reaching the very heavens: thus they will make a name for themselves. In the account of this undertaking, God is left out (as he was in the not dissimilar story of the Fall, when Adam and Eve covet the fruit of the knowledge of good and evil without prior divine sanction). The divine presence is, however, not to be permanently excluded, for God confuses their speech so that they do not understand what each is saying to the other. Their design is frustrated, and the people disperse all over the earth.

In the biblical account God is seriously worried lest an intransigent population will attain complete independence so as to eclipse his overall authority; but this is merely a primitive understanding of the divine nature. In fact, there is nothing that God, whose nature is love, will withhold from his creatures once they are qualified to use it responsibly. It is this lack of individual responsibility that thwarts our earthly endeavours, for few of us can see beyond narrow self-interest to a concern for our fellow creatures who, in our climate of enlightened ecological under-standing, include our animal and plant neighbours. When humans engage in private schemes of self-aggrandizement, the corrupting effect of power is insidious but horrifyingly final in its destruction.

Looking at the story of the Tower of Babel in more realistic terms, we can see how these ambitious people were so involved in doing their own thing that they became increasingly oblivious of the welfare of their fellow workers. In the course of time conflict soured their relationships until bitter internecine strife brought an end to the undertaking. Even if their spoken language was still mutually intelligible, the inner harmony of love was destroyed — it is not uncommon for people of different political or religious views to abuse each other, so that an outsider can see that they are simply not speaking the same language, though what they articulate is fully comprehensible to everyone. And so the project was disbanded, and the alienated population dispersed all over the country, no longer in fellowship and culturally isolated.

Every plan we make is motivated by desire; only when personal desire is well grounded in love for those around us will the action succeed in its purpose. But love comes from God, who inspires us with his love when we are quiet and receptive. Therefore we are well advised, at the end of the day, to lay open our schemes in the divine presence as we pray for guidance, and also for the strength to put into effect what we have been shown in the silence. This is not an invitation to use God in the furtherance of our private schemes — making God, as it were, our partner — but simply an admission that of ourselves we are not likely to achieve anything other than discord and final chaos. Only when the divine light illuminates our mind and the divine compassion fills our heart, can we proceed in safety, for we will know our limitations and work in trust and honesty with others on the way.

Forgive me, Lord, the many precipitate actions and summary judgements that spoil my work and hurt my relationships. Give me that knowledge of your presence that I may at once call on your help whenever some new work is to be undertaken, so that, getting myself out of the way, I may serve to the best of my ability for the benefit of all around me.

Suffering,
the Great Teacher

❖❖❖❖❖❖❖❖❖❖❖❖❖❖❖❖❖❖❖❖ ❖❖❖❖❖❖❖❖❖❖❖❖❖❖❖❖❖❖❖❖❖❖❖❖❖❖❖❖

> Let us remember for our consolation that we never
> perceive our sins till we begin to cure them.
>
> François Fénelon, *Letters and Reflections*

It is indeed true that while we are in moral disorder we tend to be
blissfully unaware of our condition. The life we are leading seems
quite adequate, our bodies are satisfactorily stimulated, and our
relationships, shoddy as they may be, are all we require. It is only
when the house we have built on the sand of transience is blown
down by misfortune that we wake up rather abruptly and start to
think about the course of our previous life. So it was with the
Prodigal Son (Luke 15.11–32), who wasted all his resources in
wanton living until everything was lost and he was in dire
destitution. Only then did he come to himself, to the full use of his
senses, and begin to survey the prospect with the calm detachment
that often follows total disaster: having nothing further to lose,
one can look into the present darkness with a freedom that is
exhilarating in its stark nakedness.

Perhaps he then considered how he had wasted his time from the
moment after he had taken his share of the family property and
squandered on ephemeral delights the money it had realized. Had
he remained in that frame of mind, his selfishness would have been
as gross as it was during the period of his debauchery. He would
simply have regretted his folly, vowing to be more careful with his
money next time in his pursuit of satisfaction. But there was to be
no next time: his destitution was too severe for that. Instead, he
had to strive for mere survival; the past was over like a bad dream
as he awoke to the terror of the present situation. And so he moved
more deeply into his condition and saw the moral poverty in which
he had lived for so long. He remembered his life at home, where
his father's servants had had more food to eat than he now had.

What was the cure that brought the sins of the young man into fine focus? It was his realization that help could come alone from his father, though the present disposition of the parent was an unknown quantity: he could quite easily have thrown his scapegrace son out of the house. And so the parental lifeline brought with it a humility previously unknown to the son, as he saw his thoughtless actions in stark perspective. He could say quite frankly, 'Father, I have sinned, against God and against you; I am no longer fit to be called your son.' These were no mere words of placation, they were the utter truth; but the Prodigal Son could never have grasped them, let alone articulated them, had he not seen his rescue ahead of him. The ultimate cure was not effected merely by his father's rapturous reception: his joy would not so much as heed any apologies in its desire for an immediate celebration. There was still the elder brother to placate, the representative of sheer justice who would not be won over by his father's outflowing love.

The conflict between justice and love is decisive, for the one may not be sacrificed on the altar of expediency for the sake of the other. We may be sure that a bad feeling prevailed between the two brothers until the repentance of the younger was substantiated in an act of positive service and sacrifice that broke down the hard-heartedness of the elder. True love, in other words, does not circumvent the demands of justice; on the contrary, it fulfils them by an act of sacrifice that hurts the giver and inspires the one who receives. It would be only then that the hard, morally correct older son would recognize the hatred lurking beneath the imposing façade of virtuous rectitude, and perhaps begin to alter his own rather rigid life-style. Hard-heartedness and rigidity effectively prevent the inflow of love into the personality, while the person remains smugly satisfied with his own perfection, as in the other great parable of the publican and the Pharisee (Luke 18.9–14). Once again the house has to be rebuilt on solid rock.

Give me the grace, Lord, to face my own shortcomings now, so that I may work whole-heartedly under your guidance for the renewal of my personality. Then I may live more fruitfully and serve more joyfully.

Aspiration in a Dry World of Discouragement

❖❖❖❖❖❖❖❖❖❖❖❖❖❖❖❖❖❖❖❖❖❖❖ ❖❖❖❖❖❖❖❖❖❖❖❖❖❖❖❖❖❖❖❖❖❖❖❖❖❖❖❖

> Not what thou art, nor what thou hast been, beholdeth God
> with his merciful eyes, but that thou wouldest be.
>
> *The Cloud of Unknowing*

Ambition is the energy that moves us on our path in life. When we are young we have time to engage in pleasant day-dreams, to escape from the material realm into fantasies of satisfaction and delight. And then comes the clamant call to immediate action, to pursue our schemes in tangible careers or occupations, so that we may both live and justify ourselves among the names of the living. Our real home may be with God from which we trail clouds of glory as we venture forth into the world of childhood and adolescence — as Wordsworth perceived in his 'Ode on Intimations of Immortality from Recollections of Early Childhood'. But we have to fashion a less beautiful home here on earth when, as adults, we can depend on nobody except ourselves to proceed with the work. It happens only too often that haste and inefficiency mar our efforts, while we may now and then fall into grosser company and betray our higher calling as humans in actions of questionable honesty and tired immorality.

> Generations have trod, have trod, have trod;
>   And all is seared with trade; bleared, smeared with toil;
>   And wears man's smudge and shares man's smell: the soil
> Is bare now, nor can foot feel, being shod.

Gerard Manley Hopkins in his sonnet 'God's Grandeur' speaks not only of the human desecration of the earth but also, more fundamentally, of the person's desecration of his or her own life in following the paths of expediency, in sacrificing moral excellence for the *mores* of the general public. One can appreciate the profundity of Jesus' baptism of repentance as a sign of his complete

26

identification with the masses, who so seldom know what they are doing to themselves and the earth on which they depend for sustenance. He remained inviolate, so radiant was the Holy Spirit within him, but we fall all too readily into temptation. The spirit may be willing, but the weakness of the poor flesh is pitiful to behold. St Paul writes, 'The good which I want to do, I fail to do; but what I do is the wrong which is against my will' (Rom. 7.19). He goes on to discover the sinful principle within us all which frustrates all our good intentions: we ourselves, by that very fact, cannot heal ourselves of this fundamental incubus. But God, in the person of his Son Jesus Christ, has placed salvation before us, since Jesus, in accepting the sin of the world and remaining uncorrupted by it, has lifted its burden from us, reconciling us once more to the Father. And so we even now, though we may often betray the highest in our reach, are still united to God, whose love sees us in the form of our distant aspirations even when our past and present actions belie our sincerity.

> And for all this, nature is never spent;
>   There lives the dearest freshness deep down things;
> And though the last lights off the black West went
>   Oh, morning, at the brown brink eastward, springs —
> Because the Holy Ghost over the bent
>   World broods with warm breast and with ah! bright wings.

Indeed, God's grandeur is, if anything, magnified by the ill-considered incursions of the human being. Our efforts, if well motivated in terms of love, bear their own reward, as do our humble lives even when our childhood ambitions remain unfulfilled. We are, as St Augustine puts it, what we love. We believe that in the fullness of time we will actualize that love in our relationships. These will last, even if the outer edifice of our works returns to the earth from which it was built.

Give me, Lord, sincerity of heart to cling to the highest I know even when the voices of the crowd occlude my deeper knowledge. May my integrity of purpose lead them quietly beyond indifference to the path of commitment where they may begin to know themselves as children of the light.

Enlightened Self-Examination

> It is a great grace of God to practise self-examination; but too much
> is as bad as too little, as they say; believe me, by God's help,
> we shall advance more by contemplating the Divinity than by
> keeping our eyes fixed on ourselves.
>
> St Teresa of Avila, *The Interior Castle*

It is an inevitable hazard of the spiritual life to harp on the weaknesses of our character to the exclusion of other, more positive, thoughts about our life and the world around us. Self-examination, to be practised especially at the end of the day, can easily lead us downwards into a dark pit of self-accusation with its attendant despair, as we see how once again we have failed in some test of charity or integrity despite all our professed vows of dedication to the higher calling of spiritual excellence. We can easily become trapped in the unpleasant, yet strangely comforting, prison of egoism. Selfishness, self-pity and self-abhorrence are part of a single complex, and once we have yielded to their noxious embrace, we can renounce hope while emphasizing our intrinsic unworthiness. The result can conveniently be termed 'negative egoism'.

Whereas the familiar 'positive egoist' has an inflated opinion of the self which soon dominates proceedings by inflicting its opinions and knowledge on the general run of the conversation, the negative egoist is engrossed in considerations of unworthiness to the exclusion of wider concerns, especially those involving the welfare of those around him or her. While we are restricted by an emphasis on the ego there can be no forward movement, no growth of the personality. Furthermore, our fill of distaste can, quite unconsciously, be projected on to other people; and so we can blame others, such as our parents, teachers, rivals, and especially the strangers in our midst, who seem to prosper while we flounder, for interfering with our own fulfilment in life.

To become rooted in oneself and one's inadequacies, no matter how sincere one's desire for change and liberation, is a certain formula for retaining them. The more we move, the more constantly do they accompany us. In the end we have to face ourself as we really are, at least in the present time, and let go completely. While it is right that we should know the situation of our inner life, we have then to acknowledge that God alone can work the marvel of change within us. All personal attempts at self-improvement simply imprison us more securely in the grip of the dominant ego. But when we take our eyes off ourself and lift them to the Lord, we are moved psychologically as well as spiritually beyond ourself to a realm of infinite love and penetrating light.

This is no short cut to spiritual proficiency, nor is it an occult technique designed to master inner difficulties. It is neither an attempt to enlist divine support in our battle with perverse tendencies, nor is it a calculated use of the divine energies for our own benefit. It is simply a humble approach to the divine throne made in complete openness and trust, and we are amazed at the response afforded us. In this state of being we can attain the Psalmist's request:

Teach us to order our days rightly,
that we may enter the gate of wisdom. (Ps. 90.12)

Therefore, as St Teresa says, we must have a balance between candid self-examination and contemplation of God. The first carried to an extreme leads to a negative egoism, while the second by itself can be a subtle way of evading personal responsibility. By ourselves we can only define our weaknesses, but when the whole personality is brought to God's care, the weaknesses are healed slowly but progressively, so that in the end they may afford us greater strength.

Lord, when I flounder in a sea of morbid self-interest, bring me to a knowledge of the problems of the wider world, so that my attention may be centred on your love rather than on my problems. May I be so released from the tyranny of my selfishness that I can provide help to anyone calling on me.

The Light on the Way
to Self-Knowledge

❖❖❖❖❖❖❖❖❖❖❖❖❖❖❖❖❖❖❖❖❖ ❖❖❖❖❖❖❖❖❖❖❖❖❖❖❖❖❖❖❖❖❖

> When thou attackest the roots of sin, fix thy thoughts more
> upon the God whom thou desirest than upon the sin
> which thou abhorrest.
>
> Walter Hilton, *The Scale of Perfection*

This observation is, to a large extent, a simple variation of the
teaching of St Teresa of Avila which we have just considered. But
there are some additional thoughts worth mentioning. Abhorrence
anchors us to the object which is hated, so that our mind can
scarcely escape from its influence. This rule applies also to personal
animosity: we cannot let the individual against whom we bear a
grudge escape our attention. In the worst instances we will expect
our friends to share our aversion, being quite angry and feeling
decidedly betrayed if they preserve their own allegiance to the
person in question. Jealousy has a similarly baneful effect: we
cannot take our minds off the unfortunate person, and are secretly
delighted if some misfortune befalls him or her.

The Italian psychotherapist and psychiatrist Roberto Assagioli
in his book *Psychosynthesis* cites a fundamental psychological
principle: 'We are dominated by everything with which our self
becomes identified. We can dominate and control everything from
which we disidentify ourselves.' It is, however, often quite
comforting to settle down behind an object of aversion; hatred can
be a most relieving emotion, and it can appear to protect us from
the necessity of coming to grips with the fullness of our character.
This applies especially to faults and vices which we can blame on
our heredity or our childhood environment. The secret of progress
in such a situation is to cease abhorring anything or anybody,
whether close to us or far away. The injunctions of Jesus come
immediately to mind, 'Love your enemies and pray for your
persecutors; only so can you be children of your heavenly Father,
who makes his sun rise on good and bad alike, and sends the rain
on the honest and the dishonest' (Matt. 5.44–5).

A well-known way out of the prison of aversion is the practice of positive thinking, in which we focus our thoughts on creative attainments while we desist from dwelling any longer on negative qualities. We evoke instead their positive counterparts. Useful as this may be in the short term, it can easily become a mere distraction; the sin is thrust underground where it continues its subversive activities.

There is, in fact, One alone who can deliver us from this savage thraldom, the God of love. The Deity is beyond the polarities of good and evil; in him is the coincidence of all opposite tendencies. This is because his nature is love, which alone can contain all qualities and transfigure them into something of the divine essence. This was seen historically in the resurrection of Jesus, whose disfigured physical body was changed to spiritual radiance, the first-fruits of the harvest of the dead (1 Cor. 15.20). In other words, when we lift up to God our thoughts about our defects and fix our entire being on him from whom all creation proceeds and on whom all life depends, we come to know him more and more and resemble him in his free acceptance. Our sins are gradually transformed by his love into qualities that are useful to us and worthy of the work lying ahead. By identifying ourselves, ever so humbly, with God who showed his nature freely to us in Jesus Christ, we can control our 'lower nature' and bring it into willing service for the benefit of our fellow creatures and the world at large.

May I know that trust in the processes of life, Lord, to lie quiet under the burden of my sins. May I know your infinite mercy so well as to offer them up without fear and as often as necessary, as my sacrifice on the altar of life. May I hold my life at all times as a potential sacrifice for my fellow creatures.

THREE

Adverse Emotions and their Healing

The Angry Heart

❖❖❖❖❖❖❖❖❖❖❖❖❖❖❖❖❖❖❖❖ ❖❖❖❖❖❖❖❖❖❖❖❖❖❖❖❖❖❖❖❖❖❖❖❖❖❖❖

> If you are angry, do not let anger lead you into sin; do not let
> sunset find you still nursing it; leave no loop-hole for the devil.
>
> Ephesians 4.26

Anger is the fourth deadly sin — the others, in sequence, are pride, covetousness, lust, gluttony, envy and sloth. And yet an emotional life devoid of anger would be tepid and unreal. Where there was no anger there might well be no strong affection either; relationships would amount to the exchange of pleasantries and a moderate overall goodwill, but with little commitment to put oneself to any trouble in helping a fellow creature.

It is certain that without anger at flaws in the prevailing system there would be no impetus for change and improvement: injustice automatically evokes anger, and then the scene is set for a reappraisal of current conditions and a move towards an equitable solution, whether in a personal relationship or in a matter of national concern. Politics would be inconceivable without the motivating force of anger, but it should always be aligned to a sensible scheme of reform. Unassuaged anger rapidly boils over into violence of speech and action, and it is here that its sinful potential becomes obvious.

The demands of Christ are radical: he extends the interdiction against murder to nursing anger against one's neighbour, abusing or even sneering at a person. Grievances have to be put right before one can bring one's gift to the altar and offer it to God, before one can offer true worship (Matt. 5.21–4). And yet Jesus' anger at the hypocrisy of the religious leaders of his time is starkly stated in the whole of Matthew 23. From all this it is clear that anger is a complex emotion and cannot be controlled by a simple set of rules. As Pascal reminds us, the heart has its reasons of which reason knows nothing (*Pensées* 4.277).

Anger seems to flow from a sense of injustice, either to oneself or to a wider community. It cannot be suppressed indefinitely, otherwise it may turn inwardly upon us and precipitate a mounting depression: some depressions are due to the anger evinced in the child by its parents, teachers or peers who acted unjustly (according to the child's set of values, which are usually very near the truth of the matter). If this emotion could not be readily expressed at the time and justice offered, the anger acts as a psychic cancer, ultimately undermining the whole inner life of the person. At this point expert psychotherapy is needed; it is futile as well as sanctimonious to preach spiritual values to a person in great psychological distress.

What, therefore, should we do when we are angry, especially when we are retiring to bed with no reconciliation in the offing? We should pray to God that our own spiritual horizon may be raised so that we may see more clearly into the disposition of those we dislike and into our own nature. It may soon come to us that we, or the system we have served, are the cause of the trouble, and until our own house is put in order there is no chance of the other person, whether individually or communally, relenting and coming to an amicable arrangement. Well does Jesus enjoin us to come to terms promptly with our legal adversary, lest far worse befall us (Matt. 5.25–6). We should, in fact, give the Almighty our anger (and all other adverse emotional responses) as our sacrifice, in much the same way as the Psalmist offers his broken spirit and wounded heart to God (Ps. 51.17). When this gift is made in good faith, the Lord does indeed accept it, and a load is, quite literally, lifted from our heart, where malign emotions tend to fester. Then we can retire to bed in peace, saying the *Nunc Dimittis* (Luke 2.29–32) with something of the thanksgiving expressed by the aged Simeon, when he saw the infant Jesus in the temple of Jerusalem. The problem assuredly still awaits solution; but at least we are in the right disposition for the verdict.

Guide me, Lord, when discord strikes anger within me, to the inner chamber of my heart, so that I may know something of your peace, which may then flow freely to all those around me.

The Healing of Anger

◊◊◊◊◊◊◊◊◊◊◊◊◊◊◊◊◊◊◊◊◊◊◊◊ ◊◊◊◊◊◊◊◊◊◊◊◊◊◊◊◊◊◊◊◊◊◊◊◊◊◊◊◊◊◊◊◊◊◊

> Better be slow to anger than a fighter,
> better govern one's temper than capture a city.
>
> Proverbs 16.32

The place of anger in our lives is a complex one. Though admittedly it is one of the 'deadly sins', to evince anger shows at least that one cares about the world. In this respect it is preferable to a spineless indifference that refuses to get involved in any controversial issue. It was the emotion of anger that set to rights many social injustices of the past; at present, conservationist groups flare up in fury when the earth is polluted by waste material, or its atmosphere is endangered by gases emitted from factories, or there is wanton destruction of tropical rain forests. Likewise those involved in the intricate matter of 'animal rights' sometimes vent their spleen on those who wear clothes made from the skins of mammals, or who are involved in scientific research that condones vivisection: attacks on laboratories may crown their activities. While one may sympathize with the concern shown in these activities, the destructive potential of the anger is disturbing in its venom and very dangerous in its effects.

The effects of unchecked anger damage not only the object of the attack but also the larger community which assesses the result from a distance. Soon many people become alienated from the cause that has inflamed the enthusiasts, who can then very easily be dismissed as emotionally disturbed trouble-makers, projecting their own inadequacies on to professionally successful people whose lives are decidedly more productive than their own. Furthermore, there is an uncomfortable amount of truth in this psychological assessment. It is evident that, while there is a place for anger in everyday life when necessary change is thwarted by selfish private interests, such an emotional reaction must be kept under careful control. The same principle holds in private affairs when injustice is being implemented, and only a vigorous reaction can put a stop to the matter.

Therefore, when one has been confronted in one's daily life by a source of discord that evokes anger, it is a good thing to examine the matter calmly in the light of cool reason. The evening is an especially good time for this exercise, since we are more relaxed then after a meal and in the agreeable surroundings of our home. Of course, if the problem is a domestic one this picture of off-work ease is irrelevant, but even here the atmosphere of rest can be of help. If we can pray in the silence of contemplation, a calm will descend on us, and Jesus' amazing injunction to love our enemies and pray for those who persecute us (Matt. 5.43–4) will become not only real but also practicable. This is because the love of God is given a chance to flow to us, and through us to all the world. We will be renewed by that love, at the same time by our very presence and the prayer that pours from us, giving it to those around us. We will be given the discernment to see how much of the trouble is due to our own inadequacy and how much to the wrong-headedness of other people; in most instances both are well represented.

Then we can proceed with calm determination to put matters right. Our restrained demeanour is much more likely to win us supporters, should these be necessary, than would violent outbursts of temper and outpourings of abuse on all those who were less certain than ourselves. In the end the wisdom of experience shows us that most problems, whether personal, communal, national or international, are settled by reconciliation in which the rights of all the parties are respected. Then each may grow a little nearer to the image of a mature person, as witnessed by the great ones of the spirit. This is something more than mere compromise, which is at most a stop-gap remedy. Compromise keeps enemies at bay, but eventually they have to undergo significant inner changes in order to work constructively together.

Give me, Lord, the self-control to harness my emotions for the good of others; and if anger is appropriate, may it be restrained and short-lived as a consequence of a drawing together of all the parties by the spirit of love.

The Dark Night
of the Spirit

❖❖❖❖❖❖❖❖❖❖❖❖❖❖❖❖❖❖❖❖ ❖❖❖❖❖❖❖❖❖❖❖❖❖❖❖❖❖❖❖❖❖❖❖❖❖❖❖❖

> If I go forward, he is not there;
> if backward, I cannot find him;
> when I turn left, I do not descry him;
> I face right, but I see him not.
>
> Job 23.8–9

Few of us escape the time of dereliction, when all around us is dark and our thoughts end in a blind alley. Existence feels like a bottomless void, and the future seems so hollow in its menacing futility that we could wish for death and a cessation of life's pain. What meaning life may have held for us has totally evaporated, and we are left with the wreckage — indeed, we are the wreckage. So did Job see himself when his life collapsed around him after disaster had struck; even his health was ruined. Jeremiah regretted the day of his birth in the throes of his suffering (Jer. 15.10), while Jesus felt totally deserted as he hung from the cross, to all present a deluded figure in a tragedy of cosmic proportions (Mark 15.33–4).

However, triumph was to crown all their suffering. The fictional Job was to see the divine presence while still alive in the flesh, but Jeremiah and Jesus were vindicated after their death. Jeremiah became something of a patron saint of the Jews during the Maccabaean uprising (2 Macc. 15.13–16), while the resurrected Christ was the focus of a new religious revelation. It is probable that the figure of Jeremiah provided the model for both Job and the Suffering Servant of Isaiah 53, later to be fulfilled in the person of Jesus.

And so, when we too are cast into darkness, we should see the experience as an opportunity for approaching and developing deeper aspects of our personality. The night time is especially taxing, for then there is no distraction from our inner misery. The way forward is to press on, regardless of what we feel. Remembering others in prayer — however hard praying may be — helps to take our attention away from ourself to the needs of our fellows. On occasions, it must be frankly admitted, prayer does become meaningless amid the enveloping gloom, and all we can do is to proceed by faith as if there was no power, no purpose, to sustain us, to guide us, other than life itself. As Bonhoeffer said, 'The only way to be honest is to recognize that we have to live in the world even if God is not there' (*Letters and Papers from Prison*).

If the condition is one of clinical depression, the relevant professional psychological aid must be sought. If the precipitating factor is the death of a loved one, we have to learn gradually to cope with the bereavement, and it is here that friends who understand the situation can be of great help — not so much by what they say as by their constant availability. To know there is someone who cares is a great boon; Job's three friends may have been useless for lightening his burden, but at least their presence helped to distract him from a despair that could have ended in suicide.

St Mechthild of Magdeburg, who lived in the thirteenth century, prayed: 'Lord, since thou hast taken from me all that I had of thee, yet of thy grace leave me the gift which every dog has by nature: that of being true to thee in my distress, when I am deprived of all consolation. This I desire more fervently than thy heavenly kingdom.' Indeed, this is the heavenly kingdom; stripped of all accessories, we can pass through the eye of the needle (Mark 10.25) to the realm beyond. It is the ultimate test, but one that confirms our humanity in general and our identity in particular.

Finally, it is always important to remember that in our desolation we are not alone: not only are we members of a greater humanity struggling to find meaning amid the chaos that befalls it day by day, but we are also in deeper communion with the martyrs of our race who died in tragedy, only to live eternally, again, like Jeremiah and Jesus, guiding us all to mastery.

May I have the faith, Lord, to face my difficulty without flinching, the perseverance to persist in the face of all discouragement, the patience to smile with all who give me unsought advice, and the love to remember those worse off than I am.

Scars of Honour

❖❖❖❖❖❖❖❖❖❖❖❖❖❖❖❖❖❖❖❖❖❖❖ ❖❖❖❖❖❖❖❖❖❖❖❖❖❖❖❖❖❖❖❖❖❖❖❖❖❖❖❖

> Though the soul be healed, his wounds are seen
> afore God — not as wounds but as worships.

Julian of Norwich, *Revelations of Divine Love*, ch. 39

In this wonderful chapter Mother Julian is shown that we are made clean by contrition, ready by compassion, and worthy by our true longing for God. These are the three means whereby all souls come to heaven; they are the three medicines by which it is incumbent on every soul to be healed. But once healing has been attained, the previous disfigurements to the personality that the sins inflicted, are not so much removed as preserved in a position of honour. The restored beauty of the person, created in the divine image and likeness, is embellished by the radiant scars of the healed wounds.

In this respect we can remember Jesus' resurrection body. On one occasion at least, the risen Lord revealed his hands and side to the disciples as they were met together behind locked doors for fear of persecution. He gave them his peace and the impress of the Holy Spirit. On this occasion one of the Twelve, Thomas, was absent, and he refused to believe the others unless he too saw the risen Christ with the signs of his crucifixion. A week later this request was granted, and Thomas's allegiance was absolute (John 20.19–29). 'Doubting Thomas' was reproved by his Lord, and has been criticized by many others since, but in fact his insistence on absolute proof was well grounded. It was the healed signs of Jesus' humiliating death, signs of disgrace rather than glory to those outside the circle of the disciples, that rendered his appearance authentic. An arresting, radiant figure claiming to be Christ might quite easily have been a demonic impersonation; but the stigma attached to his terrible death could not so easily be reproduced, because it was illuminated by sacrifice and love. Later on, the stigmata, the marks corresponding to those left by the nails and spear at the crucifixion, have been recognized as signs of great honour when they have been impressed on the bodies of occasional saints, of whom St Francis of Assisi is the most famous.

We too grow by our sins when they are fully acknowledged and given to God without excuse or justification. When we come closer to Christ, we may feel such distaste for our past actions and way of life that we speak of them only with disgust. Yet it was probably through their very disruptive effect in our lives that we came to our true being and sought the One who alone could heal us. It is always unwise to kick away the ladder on whose rungs we ascended to our present position of spiritual assurance. Each rung in its turn provided us with a small understanding of the love of God, who upheld us even when we fell into utter degradation. When we are safely in God's hands, our past misdemeanours become our means of contact with those who follow on. In this way a healed alcoholic subject can be of assistance to someone in the thraldom of this disease, in a way quite impossible for a well-wisher who has never been in contact with the condition.

In Chapter 27 of her *Revelations of Divine Love*, Mother Julian tells how she was made aware that it behoved (was necessary) that there should be sin, but that all shall be well in the end. There is a great mystery here, but one thing is clear: the sinner who repents knows the love of God, whereas the hard type of virtuous, pious person is very liable to be uncharitable to his or her less exemplary neighbour. A number of Jesus' parables and experiences in common life expound this theme, notably Luke 7.36–50, Luke 15.11–32 and Luke 18.9–14. It seems strange that we have to fall from the high ideal set within the soul before we can know God intimately; but perhaps this is the essential purpose of our perplexing life on earth. It is inevitably of limited span, but its events make their mark upon us as we prepare for the life ahead, both here and in the larger world of our dreams and of death.

I thank you, Lord, for the gift of free choice in the manner of directing my life, that I am upheld even when I have behaved foolishly, and that each experience draws me closer to your unfailing love, and therefore to my fellow creatures.

God's Presence in Adversity

✥✥✥✥✥✥✥✥✥✥✥✥✥✥✥✥✥✥✥✥✥✥✥ ✥✥✥✥✥✥✥✥✥✥✥✥✥✥✥✥✥✥✥✥✥✥✥✥✥✥

> I wish I could convince you that God is often (in some sense)
> nearer to us, and more effectively present with us,
> in sickness than in health.
>
> Brother Lawrence, *The Practice of the Presence of God*, letter 11

Of course, God is always with us, but it is we who are so often far from him. So could St Augustine lament, in his *Confessions*: 'Too late I loved thee, O thou Beauty of ancient days, yet ever new! Too late I loved thee! And behold thou wert within, and I abroad, and there I searched for thee.' It is during adversity that we tend to be drawn closer to our own being, inasmuch as the world's pleasures lift from us, and we are confronted with the one reality that will never depart, our own identity. The Prodigal Son found it in his moment of truth, and the Spirit of God within led him back to his father. He had to go a long way to find God, through many earthly vicissitudes and personal humiliations; by contrast, his cold, virtuous brother, perhaps a man of strong religious observance, was still looking for God whom he had erroneously identified with piety and duty instead of unconditional love. Where the ego is in control, there God is eased out of the picture, no matter how sincere our strivings for him may be. In the same way, the seeker after esoteric knowledge, usually pejoratively called gnosis (though there is a true as well as a false gnosis), will never find the pearl of great price until he or she has quitted all personal demands and submitted in silence to the One who is, whom we call God.

When Jacob had fled from the wrath of his swindled twin brother Esau, he spent the night at a certain place and, taking a stone to support his head like a pillow, he fell asleep. There he had his famous dream of a ladder resting on the ground with its top reaching to heaven, and angels of God going up and down upon it. The Lord was standing beside him, giving him a blessing of support, protection, and a promise of fulfilment in the form of an enormous nation inhabiting the area long after his death. When Jacob awoke, he said, 'Truly the Lord is in this place, and I did not know it.' Then he became afraid at the fearsomeness of the place, which he saw to be the house of God, the gate of heaven, calling it Beth-El (Gen. 28.11–19). Of course, God was no more present there than anywhere else, since his presence is infinite. But Jacob, himself a person of great spiritual sensitivity, was peculiarly open to the divine presence because of his fear as a fugitive.

It must be admitted that there are places where an atmosphere of great sanctity is apparent to anyone of spiritual sensitivity; places of pilgrimage come into this category, as do some, but by no means all, churches. T. S. Eliot, in *Little Gidding*, writes, 'You are here to kneel where prayer has been valid.' In such an atmosphere the reality of God is especially strong; this is the human contribution to the divine work of continuous creation in our world. Meister Eckhart boldly says, 'God can no more do without us than we can do without him.' In our little planet he needs us to put his dearest designs into practice.

If we return to Brother Lawrence's letter, we will find that he actually sees God visiting pain and sickness on us for our good. Our attitude today is very different; the ministry of healing is an important part of the Church's work. But it is right to be reminded that God is the final arbiter of all things, good and bad, fortunate and unfortunate. Later on, Jacob was to have a fight in the middle of the night with a supernatural adversary; the being, in the form of a man, wrestled cruelly with him, dislocating his hip in the conflict, but was none other than the divine presence. Jacob would not let him go until he had obtained a blessing from him (Gen. 32.24–32). Neither should we be delivered from our suffering until we have grown into better people through it. This is our blessing.

Give me, Lord, the strength and courage to go through my travail as a person of integrity, so that I may pass over from the darkness to the light, able now to guide many others on the way.

Healing and the Spirit

❖❖❖❖❖❖❖❖❖❖❖❖❖❖❖❖❖❖❖❖❖❖❖ ❖❖❖❖❖❖❖❖❖❖❖❖❖❖❖❖❖❖❖❖❖❖❖❖❖

The prayer offered in faith will save the sick man.

James 5.15

St James amplifies this assertion with further instructions: the sick
man should summon the elders of the congregation to pray over
him and anoint him with oil in the name of the Lord. He also
enjoins his flock to confess their sins to one another, and pray for
one another, and then they will be healed (Jas. 5.14–16). In these
brief instructions the basis of the ministry of healing is expounded.
The essential requirement is an openness to the action of the Holy
Spirit. The three obstacles in the way are a lack of faith in God's
healing power, a sense of guilt that makes one feel too unworthy to
be healed, and a deeper fear of being healed, possibly because of an
unconscious resistance to the demands and responsibilities of
everyday living.

Prayer, the ascent of the mind to God in aware receptivity,
always works to the extent that the divine presence is known. As
Jesus teaches us, 'Ask, and you will receive; seek, and you will
find; knock, and the door will be opened' (Matt. 7.7). The emphatic
nature of Jesus' teaching on the answer to prayer makes one think
about his own prayer in Gethsemane: he asked his Father that, if
possible, the cup of suffering might be taken away, but nevertheless
he submitted his will to that of the Father (Luke 22.41–2). Since
Jesus' work was to save, or heal, humanity by assuming its sins and
bringing them to God as a free offering, he himself had to share
fully in the pain and degradation of humanity at its lowest ebb.
'Christ was innocent of sin, and yet for our sake God made him one
with the sinfulness of men' (2 Cor. 5.21). Although Jesus' prayer
for relief was not answered, he had the power within, that of the
Holy Spirit, to survive the onslaught of immense cosmic evil. This
power was the outcome of an intense prayer life in the period
before the passion and crucifixion.

This is our paradigm of prayer for healing also. Through the
example of Jesus and his presence with us when we call upon him

44

in faith, we shall likewise receive the strength to cope with our malady. Cure is what we understandably crave, but what God wants is a total healing, so that we may manifest something of the divine image in which we were fashioned. The living example of this image is Christ himself, who is the same yesterday, today and for ever (Heb. 13.8). As this passage goes on to warn us, we should not be swept off our course by all sorts of outlandish teachings. These at their very least divert our gaze from the one from whom all true healing comes, Jesus Christ, by the power of the Holy Spirit.

Therefore in our own sickness, whether of body, mind or soul, let us first of all own up to our past faults, both to ourselves and to those around us whom we may have offended. In the primitive Christian community of St James' time there was such loving trust that each member could confess without embarrassment to the other; but we, alas, in our secular society, have to be more circumspect in revealing our confidences. Nevertheless, confession is a very important part of healing: confession both to God and to those we have hurt. Then we can be fully open to the intercessions of those who care for us, inasmuch as the emotional block of guilt is removed. The emotional release also stimulates our will to get better, because the prospect of health becomes increasingly attractive. In this way our responsiveness to God's love as manifested in the prayer of our friends, increases still further.

Finally, there is the matter of anointing with oil that has been consecrated. This reminds us that the common articles of daily usage, such as oil, water, bread and wine, receive something of God's blessing when they are dedicated to his use in humble service to our fellow creatures. There is love, as it were concentrated, in such material. The inherent holiness of matter is fully revealed.

May I so pass through my own valley of darkness, Lord, that when I emerge healed on the other side, I can give of myself freely and with understanding to all those in the throes of suffering. May my witness be a source of encouragement to the bereaved, the harassed and the outcast.

The Might
of the Holy Spirit

❖❖❖❖❖❖❖❖❖❖❖❖❖❖❖❖❖❖❖❖❖❖❖❖❖❖❖ ❖❖❖❖❖❖❖❖❖❖❖❖❖❖❖❖❖❖❖❖❖❖❖❖❖❖❖❖

> Neither by force of arms nor by brute strength,
> but by my spirit! says the Lord of Hosts.

Zechariah 4.6

The origin of this oracle comes from the post-exilic time of the Jews; seemingly miraculously they had been liberated from Babylonian exile by the munificence of the Persian conqueror Cyrus, and sent to rebuild the Holy City Jerusalem and the Temple. It was the unaided work of the Holy Spirit that had sent them home, not any feat of arms as in the first possession of Palestine under Joshua. They returned, not as triumphant heroes, but as humble stragglers, rather like the dried bones brought back to life that Ezekiel had seen in his vision some time earlier (Ezek. 37.1–14). To be sure, even the first occupation of the land had been carried out under the protective power of the Holy Spirit, but then the people were to take full charge over the country. In the second they remained subject to stronger nations, a situation destined to continue until our own time, and only after the unbearable savagery of the Holocaust.

And so the Jews returned under their governor Zerubbabel and the High Priest Joshua, to rebuild the Temple and restore national unity with all the moral integrity this implied. Despite opposition from the local tribes, who tried to undermine the authority of the Jews, the work proceeded and the second Temple, restored by Herod, was to stand until AD 70; indeed, Jesus himself valued it and taught within its precincts. The final work of restoration of national integrity was fulfilled about seventy years later by Nehemiah, under whom the walls of Jerusalem were rebuilt, and Ezra, who brought the people to a mature understanding of Judaism.

The work begun by Zerubbabel seemed small by contrast with the magnificent temple that had once adorned Jerusalem, and the people too of little significance by contrast with the stronger nations around them; but they were the nucleus around which a religion was to form that has not only stood against the ravages of time but has also been the focus of development of Christianity and Islam. The debt owed by world civilization to the twin witness of ancient Israel and ancient Greece, both very small nations in terms of the world's size, is incalculable; at their best they have represented respectively moral decency and intellectual brilliance.

And so we too learn that God has a place for us, unimportant as we may seem when we unwisely compare ourselves with other, apparently more illustrious, people in our vicinity. Even if we lack the divine spark of the acknowledged geniuses of the world, we each have a flavour all of our own: a unique personality able to give something precious to others provided we can get out of the way and let the Holy Spirit inspire us with a higher calling to personal excellence. In the glorious account of Isaiah's call to ministry (Isa. 6.1–9), after he has been divinely cleansed of sin, God asks who he should send, and Isaiah answers, 'Here I am; send me.' Most of us are called to work far less spectacular than that of God's prophet, just as not every Jew who returned from Babylonian exile was of the stature of Zerubbabel, Joshua the High Priest, or the attendant prophets Haggai and Zechariah. But each person in the new dispensation played his or her own part in the rebuilding of the Temple and the restoration of national unity.

The Temple, like all other human institutions, was of limited duration, but the faith, courage and dedication of those involved in its erection and the renewal of a vanquished people persists in the psychic atmosphere, and has inspired countless humans of later times to get on with God's particular business in their own lives. We are indeed all parts of the one body of humanity, and when we move beyond concern for personal glory, the Holy Spirit can initiate works of honour and glory with and through us.

Fill me, Lord, with such an abundance of your Spirit that I may be lifted beyond all personal limitation of thought and emotion to do the work which you would desire of me.

The Consolation
of Inner Resources

I have learned to find resources in myself whatever my circumstances.

Philippians 4.11

St Paul affirms his self-sufficiency when writing to his beloved disciples in Philippi, probably the only group that he would grace with a request for material assistance should the occasion arise. He goes on to say that he has known what it is to be brought low and to have plenty, being thoroughly experienced in the ups and downs of human existence. He has strength for anything through Christ who gives him power, but he appreciates the solicitude of his Philippian friends (Phil. 4.10–14).

It is interesting to reflect on St Paul's life. While still a zealous Pharisee, his great resource was the Law, in the pursuance of which he enjoyed persecuting the small Christian community. And then came his blinding revelation on the Damascus road that completely shattered his earlier preconceptions. It brought him to a knowledge of God as the bestower of pure grace, depending only on the will of the person to receive the divine love as revealed in the sacrifice of Jesus for the sin of the whole creation. As the apostle left behind the protecting hand of the Law, so he knew the full thrust of the Holy Spirit. Though his life became much more precarious than before his conversion, the Spirit animated him so that he knew a whole range of emotions that had previously lain dormant within him. The great rhapsody on love in 1 Corinthians 13 could not have been written by anyone who had not suffered deeply and come to know people on an intimate level of friendship.

Indeed, the Law by itself contains the seeds of death, while the Holy Spirit brings eternal life (2 Cor. 3.6). Where the Spirit of the Lord is, there is liberty (2 Cor. 3.17). This is the freedom to be oneself, to venture into the future with confidence, knowing that God is with one, sharing one's suffering no less than rejoicing in one's happiness. Like St Paul, one depends less on human support and more on the power within oneself. Paradoxically, when one is quiet and self-sufficient, one's relationships with one's fellows become smoother and more cordial, because one does not hang on to them. They feel less threatened by someone who clearly makes no persistent demands on them, but can enjoy their company for their sake alone. None of us can be completely independent — the advent of ageing and ill-health makes this embarrassingly clear — but the less we need to rely on others, the more fulfilled we become.

This is the way towards contentment. Until we are actualized as people in our own right, we will strive after material benefits to affirm our identity and demonstrate our superiority over others. But once God is the centre of our life, all earthly benefits, while not to be despised, become peripheral to our happiness. Bereavement is a constant threat in all human existence; it is experienced not only in the death of a loved one but also in a broken relationship with a spouse or close friend; and in premature retirement from work that affirmed one's importance in the social environment. And yet, again paradoxically, the experience of bereavement may be crucial to the discovery of resources within oneself that St Paul wrote about in his letter to the Philippians.

We too have to make this discovery if our lives are to be truly fulfilled. When all worldly distractions cease, then God can make his presence known. It is then that we can comply with the injunction in Hebrews 13.5: 'Do not live for money; be content with what you have.' The passage goes on to remind us of God's promise never to leave or desert us, and so we can affirm the divine assistance, having no fear of human malice. 'Poor ourselves, we then bring wealth to many; penniless, we own the world' (2 Cor. 6.10).

I thank you, Lord, for the many resources you have planted deep inside me. May they germinate in the garden of life and so flourish that I may never feel bereft despite all suffering, but rather bring comfort to those who have so little within them for consolation.

The Quality of Mercy

St Isaac of Syria, *Directions on Spiritual Training*, 85

We read in the Sermon on the Mount, 'How blest are those who show mercy; mercy shall be shown to them' (Matt. 5.7). The inner manifestation of mercy is a loosening of the grip of hard resentment. While one is in that resentful condition there can be no free outflowing of oneself to the surrounding world, for one is locked in a self-erected prison. As a result of this self-inflicted isolation one can receive little of the care of those around one; they are effectively locked out of one's personal life. And so, by extension, is God also, with the result that the life-giving Holy Spirit is slowly withdrawn from one. It is no wonder that the fifth Beatitude sees that the bestowal of mercy is the inevitable precondition of obtaining it: once we are open in forgiveness we are immediately available to the mercy of God and of our fellows also.

The principle is similar to the familiar clause of the Lord's Prayer, 'Forgive us the wrong we have done, as we have forgiven those who have wronged us' (Matt. 6.12). So the ball lies primarily at our own feet: until we have made the first move we cannot receive the divine pardon. This is not because God is recalcitrant and implacable, but because we are creatures with God-given free will which the Almighty will not override, no matter how strong the divine compassion may be for the feeble creature. How then can the impasse be breached, that it is God from whom all merciful forgiveness flows, and yet we have to initiate events?

The answer lies in our own disposition. We have first to desire to forgive, and this usually follows a sequence of events in which we have clearly done wrong or else have been in some kind of invidious, if not hazardous, situation and have been mercifully assisted by another person. This may have been a complete stranger or a disinterested colleague, or even (and most pertinently) the very person against whom we have borne the grudge. At once the bar across our own soul is unlocked and, in our relief, gratitude flows into us. It then flows out in a warmth of love that dismisses all past reservations as mere irrelevancies. The picture of the father of the Prodigal Son welcoming home the scapegrace is the perfect example: in his overflowing joy he wants only to celebrate and will hear no apologies or other expressions of repentance. The father's pain at the loss of his son was as great as the boy's pain in the throes of his destitution (Luke 15.11–32).

As St Paul puts it, 'All alike have sinned, and are deprived of the divine splendour, and all are justified by God's free grace alone' (Rom. 3.23–4). He goes on to explain this restoration of right relationship with God through God's own act of liberation in the person of his Son Christ Jesus. God was indeed in Christ reconciling the world to himself (2 Cor. 5.19). This reconciliation Christ effected by taking upon himself all the world's sin and pain, which he lifted up to the light of God's love when he was crucified and then resurrected to eternal life. And so we learn the meaning of mercy as we ourselves are rescued from death or dishonour by a miracle of grace.

Having said all this, it is nevertheless true that we do not escape the consequences of wrongful actions; God is not to be fooled, for a man reaps what he sows (Gal. 6.7). But the agent is now God and not the human: 'Justice is mine, says the Lord, I will repay' (Rom. 12.19). 'There's a wideness in God's mercy, like the wideness of the sea', as Frederick Faber puts it in a well-known hymn; and God's care never leaves the repentant sinner while paying the inevitable price for the misdemeanour. There emerges from the pit of self-imposed suffering a stronger, more compassionate person.

I thank you, Lord, for your unceasing patience in forgiving my many faults, and I pray that the light of your love will help me to erase the grudges and dark thoughts that so often cloud the charity of my soul.

The Path to Forgiveness

Then Peter came up and asked him, 'Lord, how often am I to
forgive my brother if he goes on wronging me? As many as
seven times?' Jesus replied, 'I do not say seven times;
I say seventy times seven.'

Matthew 18.21–2

This reflection follows naturally on what we have already said
about mercy and forgiveness. The forgiveness of sins is an article
in the so-called Apostles' Creed. Christians claim that they believe
in God's unceasing love which is made manifest in his action in
forgiving sins once forgiveness is sincerely sought. This sincerity
is shown in an earnest commitment to a new type of life in the
future. In this respect St Augustine's hilarious prayer, recorded in
his *Confessions*, 'Give me chastity and continence, but do not give
it yet', is soundly based both psychologically and spiritually; even if
the saint in his later severe Christianity might not have agreed with
this assessment.

What I am saying is this: we have to grow into the style of living
we desire. St Augustine knew for a long time that his hypersexuality
was a barrier to personal growth; but he also knew, however
facetiously, that he was not ready for the radical internal adjustment
that continence would precipitate. And so he unconsciously craved
for a temporary respite. One of the dangers of the spiritual life
when undertaken by those not ready for its full demands is a
humourless, rather judgemental, intensity. Inasmuch as much of
the debris in the unconscious has not been fully exposed and
appropriately dealt with, it festers inwardly and sets up a fearful
stench of decay. This may be projected on to any individual or
object that the aspirant dislikes. It is not surprising that terrible
cruelty has been committed in the name of religion; but this is a
travesty of true spirituality, which brings life in all its fullness
(John 10.10). It was, in this respect, very sad that St Augustine
could not have retained a greater respect, even gratitude, for his
pre-Christian days. His radically deprecatory view of human nature,
while not without its own truth, served to set in motion a train of

52

thought which suspected all pleasurable and sensuous emotions as the work of the dark forces. Once this puritanical view was outgrown, the sensual elements came back with a vengeance. While still imprisoned within the rigorous framework of Christianity, they spilled out in hatred and persecution.

All this has much to do with the matter of forgiveness. Despite our being aware of the desirability, indeed the necessity, of forgiving those who have hurt us in the past, despite all our prayers that our hearts should be less hard and we more open in love to all people, we find that the resentment continues to rankle. One way out of this apparent impasse is, as we saw in the last meditation, an awareness of our own sinful nature, that we are no better than anyone else: a truth borne in on us especially when we need the help of someone else after we have done wrong or are in some other position of danger. But quite often no such situation arises, and we are left with a bitterness that knows no relief.

The way to proceed then is simply to wait on God. We should not try to disguise our feelings, let alone feel guilty about them, but rather give them free rein in privacy. What is freely confronted is less poisonous than what is secreted out of propriety or guilt. If we really do desire a healing, God will give us a measure of his grace when we least expect it, and then we shall find to our joy that a terrible incubus has been removed from us. Therefore bear your burden in honest acceptance, work diligently for the well-being of your fellows, pray continually for the welfare of the world, and let go of all anxiety or self-debasement. The gift will come in the silence of self-forgetfulness. A new life will open.

I thank you, Lord, for my vibrant emotional life which responds so keenly to beauty, truth and love. May I not flinch from the pain of injustice and rejection, so that I can receive those who hate me with forgiveness and under-standing, in the end bringing them to their own understanding and acceptance.

FOUR

Love and Service

The Essence of Love

❖❖❖❖❖❖❖❖❖❖❖❖❖❖❖❖❖❖ ❖❖❖❖❖❖❖❖❖❖❖❖❖❖❖❖❖❖❖❖❖❖❖❖❖❖

As he grows greater, I must grow less.

John 3.30

These memorable words said of Jesus by the forerunner John the Baptist contain the very germ of love. To be able to stand aside and watch someone you have helped take the stage is a great privilege as well as a joy. Your work has been completed, and now you can watch the career of your charge with well-deserved pride, an emotion not to be deprecated if it is lightened with humble thanksgiving to God that you were chosen to help in his or her development. But in the Baptist's statement there is something else added: an acknowledgement of his own diminishment as he fades into the background of events, while all attention is fixed on the spiritual prodigy.

The greatest love, as Jesus says in John 15.13, is the supreme sacrifice of laying down one's life for one's friends. In fact, death is considerably easier than the slow giving up of one's possessions, so that one moves from power and worldly importance into the shadows of oblivion, there to find a final rest with the lame and the blind, the dispossessed and the discarded of the human race. And yet, strangely enough, there is a peace among the derelict that the rich and important of the world lack, of which they know nothing. So it is also at the end of the day, when the shadows of night fall and all our plans and hopes are extinguished in the comforting oblivion of innocent sleep. Sleep always brings us back to our childhood innocence, even when our daytime activities have been far from exemplary.

The drama of John the Baptist and Jesus is repeated in the lives of all caring parents. They give up their comfort, financial security and emotional stability in the cause of their children's welfare. The children grow through the glorious innocence of early childhood to the boisterous inconsideration of adolescence and the self-centred strivings of adult life, which culminate in the rearing of their own family, as the cycle is repeated through the generations. The

56

parent, at least in the mode of life of most developed countries, is something of a burden on the adult offspring, useful for caring for the very young when called upon. A cynic would also mention the final will and testament.

Any real parent, however, would laugh at this sad history, despite its factual accuracy. The joy of procreation, the supreme creative act of all living forms but invested with a special glory in the birth of a human soul, lies in the sharing of life, the participation in the growth and development of that soul to a full adult stature, and the movement out from the limited security of self-concern to involvement in something outside oneself where one can give of one's essence without reservation. One is indeed most fully oneself when one has laid aside one's self-image in burning service for one's neighbour. Whatever the future may hold, one has a stake in the life of that person, a concern that will far outlast the present time and endure until all is consummated in God.

And so the Baptist's name is eternally linked with that of Jesus; he played an essential role in preparing Jesus for his ministry by providing the baptism of repentance whereby he fully identified himself with the people he was to serve. Later, John's type of baptism was to be replaced by the more perfect baptism in the Holy Spirit of Jesus and his successors. We all have to learn that love knows when to relinquish no less certainly than when to nurture and protect. This test of humility comes to those in charge of religious communities no less than to powerful executives in the world of secular affairs. This humility becomes a humiliation only if we do not accept retirement gracefully and cannot avoid meddling in affairs that are no longer our business. But there is one consolation: a person grows more in stature for the life ahead when there is time for submission in humility, than when all revolves around his or her direction.

Give me the grace, Lord, to stand down when the time is right, and unfailingly to support my successor in personal encouragement, loyal service and constant prayer.

The Wheels of Love

❖❖

There is nothing that makes us love a man so much as praying for him.

William Law, *A Serious Call to a Devout and Holy Life*

Love, as we read in 1 John 4.7–21, is from God, and we love because he loved us first. Indeed, God is love, and he who dwells in love is dwelling in God, and God in him. Love is a divine energy, uncreated as is the divine light that shone around St Paul on the road to Damascus or in the lives of the great mystics when they were chosen, and privileged, to know the Deity as closely as any mortal may.

Love is not primarily an emotion, hard as this may be for many of us to grasp; it is simply the creative power of God renewing the lives of all he has made. It can be compared to the rays of the sun, which pour out over our solar system without remission or alteration. The clouds can shut out those rays, but the primary action of the sun goes on unimpeded — without the constancy of the sun's heat all life would be extinguished very rapidly. We love best when our minds are at rest, our emotions calm and tranquil, and our souls in such purity of regard that they can take in both the glory of God and the suffering of the world. There is no comment, no judgement, only an unreserved receptivity which can embrace all that comes to us. This state of being is rare in common life, though some of us know it at the peak of a great aesthetic or altruistic experience, when we seem to be lifted above our usual awareness to a participation in the formless glory of eternity. This state of heavenly consciousness is best called bliss, the blessedness of the soul's repose in God's care, where there is perfect joy.

To be sure, there is an emotional response to the love of God: the heart opens in unrestrained praise and a warmth flows from it that not only restores us personally but also passes to all whom we may encounter, whether in person or in thought. And so the love of God infuses the whole world when we serve in the name of God.

The essence of prayer is stillness before God. There is no passion, by which I mean a strong emotion that takes control of our minds and dominates our actions, in prayer. Until our emotions are quietened in dedicated contemplation, we cannot pray effectively. It is God who prays through us, not we who use God to influence other people according to our desires, admirable though these may seem to be, at least on the surface. When God is the master, his love pours through us, converting our hearts from stone to organs of flesh, as Ezekiel would put it (Ezek. 36.26). It is then that an affection shows itself, of a very different order to the turbulent infatuation that is miscalled love in most human relationships. Infatuation passes, to be succeeded by indifference or even dislike. The affection of God's love is constant, undemanding and of ever-widening scale, so that eventually no creature falls outside its providence.

And so, to return to William Law's observation, if we pray sincerely for a person, the love of God flowing through us will have its effect in drawing us closer to that person, even if we know him or her only slightly. Indeed, there may have been an initial antipathy between us, but constant prayer will annul it and ultimately transform it to warm affection. However, the matter is one of enlightened praying: we should not want the person to change according to our own desires, in which case we act as subtle spiritual dictators using God for our own purposes. We should enter into the trust of God's more perfect purpose, and merely beam his love into the souls of all those whom we remember in our thoughts, especially when we are quietly set at prayer.

May I know that peace of personal acceptance, Lord, whereby I can move beyond emotional attachment to outflowing service according to the demands of the present moment. May I accept myself sufficiently to receive all my fellow creatures with joyful recognition.

The School of Love

✤✤✤✤✤✤✤✤✤✤✤✤✤✤✤✤✤✤✤✤ ✤✤✤✤✤✤✤✤✤✤✤✤✤✤✤✤✤✤✤✤✤✤✤✤✤✤✤✤✤✤

When the evening of this life comes, we shall be judged on love.

St John of the Cross, *Sayings of Light and Love*, 57

The course of mortal life is strange: we appear from nowhere, receive an education, and then enter the wider world where we are fortunate to earn a living. Soon the implements of daily life take charge of us in our striving to keep alive, and they may easily assume the nature of idols. The great demand is success: that we shall have done our work well and been rewarded by the acclaim of society. This is at least as important as money, for it confirms us in our toil, giving us a sense of importance, and showing the way forward. But what is success in terms of our personal life? All our efforts fade into the background as we prepare for the final lap and retirement swallows up past achievements in a dusk of memories. We prepare for our journey to our 'everlasting home, and the mourners go about the streets', as Ecclesiastes 12.5 so poignantly puts it. Indeed, what does a man gain by winning the whole world at the cost of his true self? (Mark 8.36)

It is when we are alone in the gathering darkness of the evening that this terrible question should confront us. What have we done this day to have made our existence useful to others? If we think in terms of money and commodities we may strike a temporary abode of security, but at the heart there lies a void if human relationships have not been enriched. Things can so easily separate us from our own finer feelings and the fellowship of our neighbours. When these things disperse, we can see the residue more clearly. This is the depth of relationship we have attained with the people close to us in our family and at work. Have we acted in such a way as to foster trust and friendship, or have we simply used others as tools for our own material advancement?

Martin Buber, in *I and Thou*, writes, 'All real living is meeting.' In that coming together something of the other person attaches itself to me, as I give to him or her. In the very personal art of teaching, for instance, the teacher should not merely deliver the doctrine to the pupil, shielded by technical knowledge from direct contact. There should be an openness, an unashamed vulnerability, so that the student can question the teacher and have no compunction in pointing out the deficiencies of what has been imparted. In this way the teacher's comprehension and insight are broadened even if there is an immediate humiliation, a loss of face. But in fact something much more valuable than information has been transmitted: in the care and honesty of the encounter, the love of God has poured into the teacher's heart as the work proceeds, while the student becomes increasingly receptive to the essence of the mentor. This is out of all proportion in value to the knowledge gained; indeed, it approaches, however humbly, the unitive knowledge which is the basis of love.

Following the words quoted above, St John of the Cross adds that we should learn to love as God desires to be loved and abandon our own ways of acting.

> Loyalty is my desire, not sacrifice,
>   not whole-offerings but the knowledge of God. (Hos. 6.6)

> What is it that the Lord asks of you?
> Only to act justly, to love loyalty,
> to walk wisely before your God. (Mic. 6.8)

All the affairs of the world pass away as we quit the realm of mortal strife in sleep, and later on in the death that is the door to a new existence. In the familiar words of 1 Corinthians 13.13, 'There are three things that last for ever: faith, hope, and love; but the greatest of them all is love.' Let us therefore flow out in love to all creatures, and especially to our human adversaries, as we prepare to end this day in blessed sleep. The love will proceed even when we are asleep, as it will surely do when we 'quit this mortal frame', as Alexander Pope puts it ('The Dying Christian to his Soul').

May I be so open to your love, Lord, that I do not betray my deepest convictions in the cause of expediency, but am ready to sacrifice my life for my friends whom I may increasingly identify with humankind at large. May I be so full of love that my witness helps to raise the world from death to new life.

61

Love Never Fails

❖❖❖❖❖❖❖❖❖❖❖❖❖❖❖❖❖❖❖❖❖❖ ❖❖❖❖❖❖❖❖❖❖❖❖❖❖❖❖❖❖❖❖❖❖❖❖❖❖❖

> I have dearly loved you from of old,
> and still I maintain my unfailing care for you.

Jeremiah 31.3

This oracle comes from the incomparably great prophecy of the restoration of Israel that forms the peak of Jeremiah's ministry. He had for so long earnestly besought the recalcitrant people to repent of their apostasies and return to the Lord, in the end predicting an inevitable fall of the country to the Babylonian invaders. At that juncture he had advised surrender to the superior forces of the enemy as the only way of national survival, but his pains met only with accusations of betrayal and treason. The fate of the country was indeed sealed, and it was those who were carried away captive to Babylon that were to form the nucleus of the renewed community in Palestine after Cyrus the Persian had sent them back home.

How strange the love of God must have seemed both to Jeremiah and the survivors of the devastated community! They had broken their side of the covenant, and God's apparent wrath had descended on them. The love of God, the source of all human love, is modified by the law which controls the universe. Psalm 19 juxtaposes the law whereby the cosmos is maintained with the law that Moses brought down to the Israelites from Mount Sinai during the period of the exodus from Egypt. They are the same law, perfect in design, and there to order the whole creation aright. If the law is transgressed, punishment is inevitable. This applies to the civil law of the land no less than to the laws that control the earth's movements or the disposition of the weather. God does not alter the workings of the world to suit the creature's vagaries. 'Make no mistake about this: God is not to be fooled; a man reaps what he sows' (Gal. 6.7). The law of cause and effect cannot be revoked without a collapse into chaos of the cosmic order.

Fortunately this is not the end of the matter, otherwise the human species would long ago have disappeared from the face of the earth. We have been fashioned in the divine image, so that we are able to know God in mystical union and also to work with him in the constant creation of the world by means of our intellectual ability. When we have transgressed and suffered accordingly, our hubris is torn open, and we can at last come back to our Creator in humble penitence. The love of God is as constant as the sun's rays on our little world, and once we have left our own selfishness behind, we are able to receive the healing embrace which is comparable to the welcome home given the Prodigal Son by his father (Luke 15.22–4).

It is clear from the history of the Jews from the time of Moses and even before, that God had a special work for them to do. They were to proclaim his love and the law on which it was based, eventually forming the body of Jesus, the Word made flesh that was to reconcile all creation to its Creator. Thus Jeremiah attains a peak of inspiration with the wonderful prophecy of the new covenant between God and humanity, 'I will set my law within them and write it on their hearts; I will become their God and they shall become my people' (Jer. 31.33). This is the proof of God's love for us, his unfailing care that is still maintained even when we, in thoughtless folly, break off communication with him. It could even be said that our sad experiences of the past, once repented of in an earnest intention of doing better in the future, help to mould a finer character. A comparison with the Jews entering the Promised Land under Joshua and the remnant returning some 700 years later illustrates this theme (the matter has been discussed in 'The Might of the Holy Spirit', above, pages 46–7).

God's love never fails, since true love never comes to an end (1 Cor. 13.8). Even if our day has been a minor disaster in terms of integrity impugned and relationships damaged, we can still retire in confidence once we have confessed our sins to God. He will support us for the coming of a new day.

Lord, I thank you that you still love me when I am closed to the love of everyone. Make me so open to your love deep in my heart that I may overflow in love to everyone I meet in my daily endeavours.

Service One to Another

> When thou seest thy brother, thou seest thy Lord.
>
> Tertullian, *De Oratione*

We are told explicitly in 1 John 4.19–20, 'If a man says, "I love God", while hating his brother, he is a liar. If he does not love the brother whom he has seen, it cannot be that he loves God whom he has not seen.' But how can we see God in our brother? We cannot do it in honesty by a pure act of will, because we know that the character of the person is far removed from the perfection of God. Therefore, when we try to bring the person to God in our imagination, no matter how earnest we may be, we either delude ourselves or else are unwittingly condescending. Thus we may speak kindly of a person 'meaning well' or 'doing his or her best', when we know how flawed the performance has been, how deluded, if not ludicrously self-centred, have been the attempts to be of help.

The way forward, paradoxically, is for the time being to take our eyes off the person (who is both our neighbour and our brother), and enter into the quiet silence of God. This is called contemplation, and it is attained by a dedicated attention to the present moment. In this state the mind is lifted up to God, who in turn lifts us up when our disposition is God-centred. By this is meant a giving of our very selves to the highest we may know in terms of the three ultimate values: beauty, truth and goodness. As we approach the divine presence, a peace enfolds us in which all discourse is taken up into the fellowship of God. We worship, as Moses did at the peak of Mount Sinai, and the divine energies pour into our feeble frames, transfiguring our very being. 'And because for us there is no veil over the face, we all reflect as in a mirror the splendour of the Lord; thus we are transfigured into his likeness, from splendour to splendour; such is the influence of the Lord who is Spirit' (2 Cor. 3.18).

As we descend from our own mountain of transfiguration, we carry the love of God with us. The light shines from us as a warmth that excludes no one from its concern. In rather the same way as the spiritual radiance of Jesus enlightened the drab faces and even duller minds of the many people he met in the course of a day's work, and lifted up to caring responsibility the coarse sensuality of the sinners with whom he dined, so, to a much smaller extent do we impart something of the divine peace we have received to our neighbours in the throes of their own travail. We may even set aflame the spark of divinity in them by the heat of our presence. It is thus that we begin to see 'the real light which enlightens every man' that was fully incarnate in Jesus (John 1.9).

It is then that we can truly begin to love our brother, since the love of God flows impartially to all around us, irrespective of their moral character or personal life-style. Love, like God, has indeed no favourites (Acts 10.34); this is the difference between love and affection. In the love of God we can identify the other person with ourself, including the outer surface scarred with its own infirmities. Only when we can so accept and love ourself can we equally accept and love our brother; the One who first loves us all is God: we love because he loved us first (1 John 4.18).

And so we should serve our brother as we would our Lord. This was the lesson taught by Jesus to his disciples when he washed their feet just before his betrayal and passion. He identified himself with their uncleanness in order to infuse them with his holiness. Only thus is the creature accorded his or her full stature in the world of eternal values. 'And indeed this command comes to us from Christ himself: that he who loves God must also love his brother' (1 John 4.21).

May my life be so dedicated to your service, Lord, that I can see the light of Jesus reflected in the faces of all who pass my way. May that light so infuse my own life that I become an instrument of your love to the world around me.

Sensitivity in
our Neighbour's Pain

❖❖❖❖❖❖❖❖❖❖❖❖❖❖❖❖❖❖❖ ❖❖❖❖❖❖❖❖❖❖❖❖❖❖❖❖❖❖❖❖❖❖❖❖❖❖❖

> The heart knows its own bitterness,
> and a stranger has no part in its joy.
>
> Proverbs 14.10

How very alone we are indeed when tragedy strikes! There may be
no dearth of well-wishers, and well-doers too, but somehow their
very presence irritates rather than comforts. We may be sure that
they mean well, but their solicitude somehow grates on our inner
feelings, and how relieved we are when they have departed after
having said and done their expected piece! This is, of course, very
unkind, and when we have risen above our irritation, we have a
chance to see ourselves in similar circumstances, bestowing our
attention on others with appropriate concern and then moving on,
in our own hearts thankful that we have not suffered likewise, and
then deflecting our thoughts along more profitable channels.

> Go, go, go, said the bird: humankind
> Cannot bear very much reality.
> Time past and time future
> What might have been and what has been
> Point to one end, which is always present.

These lines come from 'Burnt Norton', the first of T. S. Eliot's
Four Quartets. We cannot bear much reality because we are not
able to live in the perpetual now, the present which we can alone
acknowledge and affect. The past is a repository for used
experiences on which we can reflect, perhaps with cold resentment
or else sweet nostalgia. The future is a menacing realm of test,
trial, failure or success depending on outer circumstances and
inner strength. If only we could, like the twelve-year-old Jesus, be
unceasingly about our Father's business (Luke 2.49), we would be
centred completely in the present moment, which is both the final

66

summary of the past and the controlling-point of the future. And then we would be able to share authentically and constructively in the woes and joys of other people.

The heart of the matter is this: until we can get ourselves out of the way, we cannot relate effectively to other people. While our thoughts are centred on ourselves, our time, our reputation, the image we are showing, and a score of other personal matters, we cannot be one with the other person. When all is going well, we can pass off our superficiality amid the light conversation of the passing hour, but when a deeper response is required, we will feel embarrassed at our helplessness, and so quickly revert to platitudes to conceal our naked shallowness.

The bitterness of which the writer of Proverbs writes may be a personal disappointment rather than a major tragedy, and here the privacy of the wounded heart is even more precious. The victim comes to realize that much solicitude has unconscious elements of condescension about it. The well-wisher unintentionally places himself or herself on a level above the sufferer, from which sage advice and reassurance can be given. The picture of Job's three well-intentioned friends comes to mind; they meant to comfort Job, but merely irritated him still further because of their insensitivity.

And here we reach the core of participation in the life of another person, whether in sorrow or in plenty. Only when we have attained such inner silence that we do not feel embarrassed at our lack of words and gestures, can we know some of the sufferer's bitterness, because it resonates with our own experience. And what we ourselves lack in knowledge is available in the life of Jesus, who, like the Suffering Servant of Isaiah 53, 'had no beauty, no majesty to draw our eyes, no grace to make us delight in him'. As we share in the common human lot, so this servant will come closer to us, and we to those who are in pain. A true friend knows the disposition of another's heart; if we have even one such friend we are truly blessed by God.

May I have the sensitivity, Lord, to be a source of comfort to my suffering neighbour by giving my very essence to relieve the pain and set the tortured mind at rest. May I have the inner joy to relish another's good fortune and to add to its celebration.

Loving our Neighbour as Ourself

❖❖❖❖❖❖❖❖❖❖❖❖❖❖❖❖❖❖❖❖ ❖❖❖❖❖❖❖❖❖❖❖❖❖❖❖❖❖❖❖❖❖❖

> Anything you did for one of my brothers here,
> however humble, you did for me.
>
> Matthew 25.40

This quotation forms the first peak of the Parable of the Sheep and the Goats (Matt. 25.31–46). It asserts that when the Son of Man comes in his glory, he will separate humankind into two groups. One will consist of those who have cared for their fellows in such everyday concerns as providing food and drink, caring for the stranger and the sick, and visiting the prisoner; whereas the other will have neglected these basic works of charity. We are told that whoever cares for even the most degraded of his or her fellows is also caring for Christ and has his Father's blessing; those who reject a fellow creature also reject the Lord, and are promised eternal punishment. The righteous enter eternal life. The parable is especially poignant, because Jesus identified himself with the most degraded criminals on the cross and no one came to his succour. The three women at the foot of the cross showed up best, for at least they supported him invisibly with their love (John 19.25).

There are two types of 'sheep': the one helps other people with an eye to future rewards in the life beyond death, and the other genuinely loves humanity, and indeed all created things. It is important to understand that performing a kind action is its own reward, for somehow one has been lifted from a narrow enclosure in one's own personality to a participation in the life of the world, whose Creator stands aloft as a loving father. And so kindness is not premeditated with an eye to future results, but is a spontaneous outflowing of love to our neighbour as we are about our daily business. To do the work commended in this parable, we have to be so aware of the present moment, so undistracted by thoughts, that

68

we are in psychic communion with the person in need. The Parable of the Good Samaritan is our model here: while the priest and Levite walked past the assaulted man on the other side of the road, the lowly, disregarded Samaritan could identify himself immediately with the victim's plight and act accordingly (Luke 10.30–37). The uncharitable person is preoccupied with his or her own concerns, whereas the loving person has passed beyond self to God. 'We for our part have crossed over from death to life; this we know, because we love our brothers' (1 John 3.14). And so the very act of caring for another being means that the love of God is pouring through us.

There are two further thoughts. The resurrected Christ showed himself to two disciples on the Emmaus road in the person of a stranger, who first engaged them in learned discussion before revealing himself at the breaking of bread (Luke 24.13–32). Had they not been so bereft, they might well have disregarded the man. We are often more open in love when we have little to give materially. And secondly, we all fail from time to time in rendering the service demanded by the Parable of the Sheep and the Goats. We all have our breaking-point, and we have to learn our limitations. Once service becomes obsessional it soon kills the springs of compassion within us, and God's love becomes a burden rather than a blessing. This is why it is so important to work in a group, of which the Church is the model.

Let us finally remember the wise words of St Seraphim of Sarov: 'Man must be lenient with his soul in her weaknesses and imperfections, and suffer her failings as he suffers those of others, but he must not become idle, and must encourage himself to better things.' This is the essence of love: to accept people as they are in order to direct them to what they are to be. This God alone knows, but our image is Jesus Christ.

I pray, Lord, that I may never be so preoccupied with my own affairs that I become oblivious of the greater demands made on me as a neighbour and a citizen, to help those in need and to take my stand in the cause of justice and reconciliation.

Loving Ourself
as our Neighbour

❖❖❖❖❖❖❖❖❖❖❖❖❖❖❖❖❖❖❖ ❖❖❖❖❖❖❖❖❖❖❖❖❖❖❖❖❖❖❖❖❖❖❖❖❖❖❖❖❖❖

We should be in charity with ourselves as with our neighbours.

François Fénelon

This advice is the reverse side of the second great commandment, to love our neighbour as ourself (Lev. 19.18, and repeated by Jesus most memorably in connection with the Parable of the Good Samaritan in Luke 10.25–37). To love oneself may appear not only unrealistic but also indulgent, especially when, at the day's end, we have time to consider our behaviour earlier on. St Paul, in Romans 7.14–24, bemoans the divided consciousness so typical of the human: we tend to do what we inwardly detest and fail to do what we outwardly acclaim. Indeed, the more we try to ascend to God in prayer, the more firmly do our shortcomings anchor us to the earth. We may make earnest resolutions to do better in future, only to find how easily we revert to accustomed ways of behaviour.

It is important to understand how our sincere strivings for self-improvement tend to be frustrated by the assertive ego. It looks for results to the extent of neglecting wider social concern. It can easily thwart our spiritual progress. The way forward is by learning to let go, ceasing to judge ourself either adversely or favourably. To rest in one's own being is the beginning of self-love. It gives one a breathing-space in which to let outside events claim our attention. The more unattached we are to ourself, the more we can survey our inner life calmly, and see what is causing the trouble; in fact, it is the Holy Spirit within that is revealing the truth to us, for in this state of suspended judgement and psychic awareness the divine presence can enter the soul to full acclaim. It is like a glow of warmth animating us when the sun's first rays lighten the surrounding air in the chill of a winter's morning.

The power of the Holy Spirit enables us to survey ourselves dispassionately, at the same time accepting that all is well in the mind of God even if in the beginning we may feel disheartened by the release of previously controlled emotions of adverse quality. We learn that we are infinitely lovable, despite — or even because of — our infirmities. God loves us because he made us: this statement is the key to our relationship with God, but it remains something of a theological postulate until we have experienced that love when we were cast down in darkness. We can be in charity with ourselves only when we know that someone greater than we are both understands us and cares for us: in practice, God in Christ alone fulfils this criterion. When that love fills us, we at once radiate it to those around us, so that we can genuinely love our neighbour as ourself. Until we genuinely love ourself, we cannot love anyone else because the love of God cannot penetrate us and make us effective agents in spreading that love.

So therefore relax at the end of the day and let good humour pervade you. We can be so concerned about our neighbour that we neglect ourself instead of loving both equally. If we face ourself squarely, we will probably see little obvious improvement in personality over the years until we suddenly note a change of attitude to a particular situation. Even the spiritual giants have their 'off days'; so therefore smile indulgently at your weaknesses. Not to be in charity with oneself is a type of spiritual pride.

It may be true that happiness lies more in giving than in receiving (Acts 20.35), but there is also a peculiar graciousness in being able to receive gladly; self-sufficiency, whether material or spiritual, can degenerate into pride if it is incapable of accepting assistance. Likewise, in times of prayer it is important to be quiet and receive the love of others remembering us, and not simply be giving out the whole time.

May I attain that inner tranquillity, Lord, in which I can see my attitudes dispassionately and evaluate my actions kindly in the face of the turmoil around me. May your love so fill me with new resolve that I can give of myself with confidence as well as compassion to the service of the world.

71

Loving God
and our Neighbour

❖❖❖

We cannot know whether we love God although there may be
strong reasons for thinking so, but there can be no doubt
about whether we love our neighbour or no.

St Teresa of Avila, *The Interior Castle*

The problem of this statement lies in the tortuous quality of so
much human emotion. Jeremiah was only too correct when he
lamented the deceit and moral sickness of the human heart (Jer.
17.9). St Paul, in a rather similar fashion, showed how we are so
often governed by emotions contrary to what we desire in our
times of decision (Rom. 7.19). There is a type of strong positive
emotion, commonly called love, which is in fact an uncontrollable
desire to possess another person, to overwhelm and take charge.
Once this desire has been satisfied, the object of infatuation is
likely to be imprisoned in a passionate embrace that prevents any
further independent movement. This terrible state of affairs may
continue indefinitely, depending entirely on the selfish needs of the
'lover'; on the other hand, the object of this lustful desire may be
summarily discarded like a piece of old clothing once the emotional
attraction has faded. The love of Don Juan is of this character, and
the emotional pain visited on the victim may be of suicidal intensity.
(The matter has been further discussed in 'The Wheels of Love',
above, pages 58–9.)

It seems evident that a love which has a strongly passionate
component has to be treated with firm discretion. The test is its
durability, and whether it allows the object of affection sufficient
freedom to carry on his or her own life without interference. It is
on this note that a more mature love can be discerned. It is a warm
desire for fellowship, for mutual protection, and finally for union.
It tends to grow in the breadth of satisfaction until the desire
begins to fade away and the union becomes firm, even rock-like in
commitment. And then love of a noble maturity flows between the

two participants, and from them to an ever-increasing number of other people.

When we see love in this context, it is evident that St Teresa's certainty about our love, or our lack of it, for our neighbour needs careful qualification. But St John is equally emphatic: 'If a man says, "I love God", while hating his brother, he is a liar. If he does not love the brother whom he has seen, it cannot be that he loves God whom he has not seen' (1 John 4.19–20). But immediately preceding this passage is the pivotal statement that we love because God loved us first.

In fact, you know that you are at least starting to love your neighbour when your heart, or inner being, opens to him or her, and compassion joins you to the person. There is a spontaneous giving of yourself to that individual, which is in fact the love of God flowing through you to him or her. The concept of flow is especially apt, because love is an uncreated energy of God, as is also the uncreated light described in 2 Corinthians 3.7–18. It is not associated with any emotional outpouring, but when it flows through us, it evokes a warmth of affection that not only changes our heart of stone into vibrant flesh, but also enlightens our mind, so that we can see much of what is invisible to the naked eye and incomprehensible to the native intellect. It is in this respect that we can know that we are deeply concerned about our neighbour, as the Good Samaritan was in his famous encounter with the robbed, assaulted traveller on the Jericho road. If we can see love in this context we will not be far from God at any time; for the more his love flows through and from us, the closer we are both to him and to our neighbour. The more we love God, the more does that love overflow to those around us. Conversely, if we love our neighbour in undemanding solicitude, we will draw ever closer to the knowledge of God. The all-important discipline is prayer; this brings us unceasingly close to God and his creation.

May I have, Lord, that steadfast attention to the work of the present moment that will make me ever aware of the needs of those around me, so that I may be an unfailing instrument of your love in whatever situation I may find myself.

❖❖❖❖❖
FIVE
❖❖❖❖❖

*Wisdom and
Personal Integrity*

Faith in the
Service of Understanding

Understanding is the reward of faith. Therefore seek not to
understand that thou mayest believe, but believe that
thou mayest understand.

St Augustine, *St Julius Gospel*

Faith is the basis of all human endeavour. It gives substance (or
assurance) to our hopes, and makes us certain of realities we do not
see (Heb. 11.1). If we did not have faith in the rational running of
the universe, we could not plan our day-to-day activities. If the
scientist did not have faith that the phenomena being investigated
were rationally organized, his scheme of research would be random,
not merely ill-conceived but devoid of all credibility. Since the
human mind is a powerful intellectual organ, it can work creatively
in a milieu of intelligence, both discovering new facts and moulding
the outside world progressively to suit its own concerns. As we are
all learning, perhaps too late, the organizing power of the human
can be disastrously selfish, destroying in the process of its activities
vast expanses of nature, polluting the atmosphere, and finally
precipitating its own destruction. It is a sobering thought that
unqualified understanding can lead to wholesale suicide.

But there is a higher, nobler faith, the resolution to stand or fall
by the noblest hypothesis. This definition was propounded by
Frederic Myers, a nineteenth-century scholar and poet, who was
also concerned about the rational investigation of psychical
phenomena. Such faith involves values, the three ultimate ones
being truth, beauty and goodness (or love). There is no fundamental
reason to believe that any one of this triad is authentic; certainly
there is often a triumph of falsehood, ugliness and cruelty in our
human counsels. And yet we are all strangely attracted to the great
philosophical and spiritual ideals inherent in the world's higher
religions; even hardened criminals have their own code of justice,
unless they are so mentally disturbed as to be incapable of moral
judgement.

This higher, nobler faith seems to be a natural quality of the soul. Tertullian wrote, 'O witness of the soul naturally Christian' (*Apologia*, 17), and until we realize the Christ presence within us, we can never be whole people. In the process there may have to be immense suffering, so that the worldly idols that cloud our faith with false understanding, the wisdom of man which is less wise than the foolishness of God (1 Cor. 1.25), are cleared from our vision. Quoting again from Tertullian, 'The more they mow us down, the more we grow; the seed is the blood of Christians' (usually rendered, 'The blood of the martyrs is the seed of the Church'). The writer of the Letter to the Hebrews, in chapter 11, celebrates the acts of faith of the saints of the Old Testament: against all odds they followed the inscrutable calling of God, and later they understood more and more of the divine purpose; but, like all of us, they had to wait until they died to see the full import of what they had done in pure faith.

In our own lives we may have to proceed in darkness, sometimes acting in a way quite inconsistent with what our peer group, even our family and closest friends, would expect of us. How fortunate we are if we have even one soul friend, a genuine spiritual director, to encourage us on the path! But if we follow the noblest way, learning to get ourselves out of the picture, like the Blessed Virgin Mary, the prophets of Israel, and Jesus himself at Gethsemane, we will understand. Every experience is here to bring us closer to our own completion, which is Christ in (and among) us, our hope of a glory to come (Col. 1.27). Tertullian once again stretches us: 'It is certain because it is impossible' (*De Carne Christi*). For what is impossible for humans is possible for God (Luke 18.27).

Help me, Lord, to be diligently about my business, ever aware of your voice calling me on to new endeavours. Even when I am led into an untravelled path may my faith hold firm, confident that in the end I will see you more fully and do whatever else you require ever more worthily.

Doubt in the
Service of Faith

❖❖❖❖❖❖❖❖❖❖❖❖❖❖❖❖❖❖❖❖❖❖ ❖❖❖❖❖❖❖❖❖❖❖❖❖❖❖❖❖❖❖❖❖❖❖❖❖❖❖❖

Why did you hesitate? How little faith you have!

Matthew 14.31

These were the words of Jesus in the context of his walking on the water. The disciples were in their boat some distance from the lake shore in the middle of the night, when a sudden squall assailed them. Jesus himself had stayed behind on the hillside to pray alone. When he was aware of the disciples' trouble he walked over the lake towards them, and they were terrified, thinking they were seeing a ghost. Once he had identified himself, Peter wanted complete assurance, and asked his Master to summon him alongside. As soon as Jesus complied with this request, Peter stepped down from the boat, and walked over the water towards him. But the sheer strength of the gale brought poor Peter down with a vengeance: his terror separated him from Jesus, and he realized how precarious, indeed impossible, was his situation. And so he began to sink, and called out in terror to be saved. At once the Lord reached out and caught hold of him; they climbed into the boat, and the storm subsided. The disciples were struck with awe, and acknowledged Jesus' greatness (Matt. 14.22–33).

This incident can tell us much about faith in action and also about the place of doubt. A notorious schoolboy definition of faith is believing something you know is untrue. Few of us, however pious we may be, would go as far as that, but quite a few believers feel that the slightest questioning of the credal basis of their religion is sacrilegious. Because their own stability depends on a rigid affirmation of all the articles of their faith, they are soon liable to persecute any waverers. One outcome of such unchallengeable faith is fanaticism, another is superstition: if a person does not act according to the rules, God is sure to punish him or her with misfortune.

Such a faith may sustain one temporarily, but in due course a

78

situation will arise to test that faith to the point of breaking. So Job's previous confidence in God's providence according to the traditional Wisdom teachers of the Old Testament, was shattered when he saw that righteous living was no assurance of good fortune. The writer of Ecclesiastes could see no obvious relationship between virtue and providence — the book is a masterpiece of doubt, but it tells us to get on with our life as best we can, living completely in the present moment; if we expect special treatment for our efforts, we are liable to disappointment. Experience teaches us that doubt is the mortar that binds together the bricks of faith in the foundation of a house that can withstand the pounding of the misfortunes of life. Without that reinforcement the house would soon collapse at the onslaught of life's unruly elements (this is an unusual application of Matthew 7.24–7, truth being the reconciling quality between Christ's words and honest doubt).

There is, however, a type of faith quite essential in daily living. It is the courage and tenacity to proceed with the work in hand despite the discouraging wisdom of both the bystanders and our own critical mind. When we are involved in purposeful action, the key to success is self-forgetfulness and concentration on the present situation: no one who sets his hand to the plough and then keeps looking back is fit for the kingdom of God (Luke 9.62).

In the episode that sparks off our meditation, it was the immense spiritual power flowing through and from Jesus that supported Peter, but once he yielded to his rational mind, Peter blocked that power of the Holy Spirit and at once began to sink. So do we also if we cut off the power of God by failing to trust in times of trial. But if we can persevere despite all misfortune, we shall enter a new realm of human activity, energized by the love of God.

> There's no discouragement
> Shall make him once relent
> His first avowed intent
> To be a pilgrim.

May I have the humility to forget myself, Lord, as I prepare to yield my spirit to you each night in sleep; so that, when the time of trial afflicts me, I may be so perfectly obedient to your Spirit that together we may do the work which is required of us.

The Quest for Wisdom

Teach us to order our days rightly,
that we may enter the gate of wisdom.

Psalm 90.12

In this penetrating psalm the writer meditates upon the eternity of God and the transience of human existence — seventy years is the span of our life, eighty if our strength holds; upon God's power and human weakness; upon the wrath of God and our own frailty. In the face of the terrible majesty of the Creator, we learn by bitter experience that of ourselves we are nothing, that God can turn us back to dust whenever he chooses. And so we begin to see our lives more clearly as they are divested of their apparent power and importance. As age proceeds we may be relieved of many of our possessions and find our personal importance a faded relic, but in the emptiness of worldly things the Spirit of God has a greater opportunity to make an unhurried, undramatic entry into our being. There he teaches us wisdom, which may be defined as an embracing understanding of our place in the total scheme of things, of what we are here to achieve, and of what we are to become in the greater life beyond mortal death.

Wisdom is an understanding of a very different order from knowledge, which is concentrated, specialized and transient, inasmuch as its contours are forever changing as more facts are known and past misconceptions corrected. There seems to be no end to the research that brings with it greater knowledge; as St Paul would put it, 'our knowledge and our prophecy alike are partial, and the partial vanishes when wholeness comes' (1 Cor. 13.9). The wholeness he writes about is a wisdom that can embrace the discrete facts of worldly life, including scientific research, and bring them into a wide context of human growth and spiritual development. Knowledge is the commodity of the specialist whereas wisdom knows no intellectual barriers except the capacity to be silent, aware and deeply understanding. It may be present in an inconspicuous worker who has experienced life deeply, while absent from the intellectual giant who has formed few relationships outside the professional milieu acquainted with the work in question.

The true beginning of wisdom is the desire to learn, we read in Wisdom 6.17. The passage goes on to say that a concern for learning means love towards wisdom, a love that means keeping her laws, the observance of which guarantees immortality, which in turn brings a person closer to God. The desire to learn is a product of humility, a state of mind usually brought about after our illusions of self-sufficiency and importance have been torn away by suffering of one type or another. It is one thing to learn a particular discipline with suitable professional training; the result is knowledge. It is quite another matter to learn wisdom, for life itself is both taskmaster and teacher. If we are fortunate we may meet wise counsellors on the way, but they are there essentially to encourage and direct us, so that we may proceed on our unique path in silent awareness and firm dedication.

The exquisite Wisdom poem of Job 28 ends with the dictum,

The fear of the Lord is wisdom,
and to turn from evil is understanding.

This fear is an awe in contemplating the immensity of the universe and the majesty of its Creator. The wrath of God mentioned in Psalm 90 is the law by which creation is maintained, a law written into the cosmos no less than into the human soul in terms of the moral imperative to righteousness. Its essence is the Ten Commandments, and to obey them is to begin to order our days rightly, that we may enter the gate of wisdom.

But something else is needed for us to pass through the gate into the fair country beyond. This is a love of such dedication that we are prepared to give up our very life for our friend (John 15.13), who in the final analysis is everyone around us. Love completes wisdom as it fulfils the whole law.

May I have the vision to live justly with my neighbours now, Lord, so that I may gradually attain the wisdom that comes with experience, is fertilized with love, and pours down in blessing to all whom it touches.

The Wisdom of Tolerance

❖❖❖❖❖❖❖❖❖❖❖❖❖❖❖❖❖❖❖❖ ❖❖❖❖❖❖❖❖❖❖❖❖❖❖❖❖❖❖❖❖❖❖❖❖❖

O God, help us not to despise or oppose what we do not understand.

William Penn

Deep within us all is the desire for security; no doubt, it has its roots during our experience in our mother's womb and later in our earliest infancy, when we could depend absolutely on the outside environment and the care of our parents for our sustenance. Even this statement has to be qualified by the acknowledgement that not all pregnancies are harmonious and not all families happy, a circumstance only too obvious when we think of the many one-parent families in our midst nowadays. Certainly, the more secure we have been in the love of our own parents, and the more effortlessly we have entered into the *mores* of our peer group later on, the more able we are to accept ourselves as we are, taking both ourselves and our environment for granted. The ignorance that is a part of childhood is gradually eased away by the experience of adolescence and the deepening furrows of adult life: 'When I was a child, my speech, my outlook and my thoughts were all childish. When I grew up, I had finished with childish things' (1 Cor. 13.10–11).

We should never lose the breathless receptivity and wonder of childhood innocence, remembering that 'whoever does not accept the kingdom of God like a child will never enter it' (Mark 10.15); but the inevitably limited understanding of the young has to be broadened by the chequered course of life. In this way sharp judgement is informed by deeper compassion, naive certainty by questioning faith, as deeper aspects of existence force themselves upon us. To be shown that one's view on a particular matter is simplistic if not frankly ill-informed constitutes an intolerable loss of face for the person who is emotionally immature, but affords a breath of fresh air to the healthy seeker who is prepared to sacrifice all personal comfort in the pursuit of truth.

'Do not stifle inspiration and do not despise prophetic utterances, but bring them all to the test and then keep what is good in them

82

and avoid the bad of whatever kind' (1 Thess. 5.19–22). Here St Paul is warning his disciples not to quench the power of the Holy Spirit but the same caution applies to all insights and styles of living that are at variance with the norm. Tolerance is a feature of the well-centred person, but it can also drift dangerously into a thoughtless, indeed careless, permissive attitude that refuses the challenge of value judgements. Jesus warns us neither to judge nor condemn another person, an attitude he himself maintained in the case of the woman caught committing adultery (John 8.11), but he also reminds us that a person's actions and manner of life are recognized by their fruits (Matt. 7.15–20).

It is here that William Penn's noble prayer quoted above, finds its answer. Let us be quiet and flow out in goodwill to all new ventures even when their protagonists disturb our sense of convention; to be unshockable is the prerequisite of the effective counsellor. In this way our own adverse emotions are effectively checked as we enter into a deeper spiritual rapport with the person and his or her works. It is in the depths of such a relationship that the Holy Spirit can clear our minds of prejudice while bringing them to a clarity of perception in which we can see the fruit in terms of truth, beauty and goodness. St Paul's list of the harvest of the Holy Spirit is an especially helpful guide: 'love, joy, peace, patience, kindness, goodness, fidelity, gentleness and self-control' (Gal. 5.22). As we develop these fruits, so we can apply them to all that is aberrant and unclean, following the way of Jesus himself amongst the crowds of his time. At the same time we can respond in joyful recognition to the truth, beauty and goodness that we encounter in the new thing, exulting in its own integrity.

Give me, Lord, the humility to stay silent and to listen in courtesy and respect to the voices of the throng, so that I may learn more about myself as a preparation for more effective service.

Wisdom and Experience

> How good it is for me to have been punished,
> to school me in thy statutes!

Psalm 119.71

We do indeed learn by experience. In our callow youth (of inexperience rather than mere years) we tend to live on a surface level punctuated by the routine of daily duties. This is especially so when all goes well with us. We take our good fortune for granted as we proceed heedlessly along, moved essentially by our own selfishness.

> You may listen and listen, but you will not understand.
> You may look and look again, but you will never know.
> This people's wits are dulled,
> their ears are deafened and their eyes blinded,
>   so that they cannot see with their eyes
>   nor listen with their ears
>   nor understand with their wits,
> so that they may turn and be healed.

Isa. 6.9–10, quoted in Matt. 13.14–15, John 12.40 and Acts 28.26–7

This impervious attitude is not willed by God, as a superficial reading of these texts might lead one to think, but is a part of the consciousness of the human in a state of spiritual ignorance, and has been anticipated by God. Until there is a greater awakening, the faculties of sensation and the working of the mind will be limited to purely surface interests.

In due course the heedless gallop draws up to a sudden halt. The cause of this arrest may be a bodily injury that followed a thoughtless action when the mind was not attending to the present moment. It may, on the other hand, be a disease coming after persistent abuse of the body by smoking, alcohol or drugs. It may instead be an equally precipitate break in a personal relationship that we had taken for granted, but were completely unaware of a friend's or business partner's growing restiveness. Alternatively

84

there may be a breakdown of marriage. The infidelity of our partner may assail us as a bitter blow, so that we vent our spleen by citing with wrath the seventh of the Ten Commandments. But when the emotional discharge has had its place, we are forced to be quiet and turn our gaze inwards. (The matter has also been discussed in 'Suffering, the Great Teacher', pages 24-5.)

So did the cruel, lustful David after his seduction of Bathsheba and the cunning murder of her noble husband Uriah; Nathan confronted him to his face with his wickedness by means of a parable, and said, 'You are the man' (2 Sam. 12.7). Likewise did Elijah the perfidious Ahab after he had had Naboth murdered in order to acquire his vineyard. David, a man of considerable moral stature, repented and prevailed, but only after terrible internecine strife within his own family. The far less worthy Ahab was soon to be killed in battle. Peter was confronted starkly with his cowardice when on three successive occasions he denied all knowledge of his Master. But the terrible affliction that followed this self-knowledge was healed by the forgiveness of the resurrected Christ.

Until we have come into relationship with the Law of God, we have not come of age spiritually. Many of us need a conflict with that Law before the sinfulness lying within us can be exposed, confronted, and then given to God in humility and faith as our little sacrifice.

Nothing in our life is simply eradicated, though we may pathetically believe it to have been. It will recur in due course until it is given to God. Then alone can it be cared for and healed by the divine compassion. And so it comes about that God's statutes are given to us so that we may attain that perfect life shown to us by Jesus himself, who did not come to abolish the Law and the prophets, but to complete them (Matt. 5.17). Through him we now know that the fulfilment of all the statutes of the Law is love (Rom. 13.10). When one has known affliction personally, one can comprehend another's weakness and suffering, and be open to that person in compassion. Through the open, tenderly palpitating heart God's love can flow.

I thank you, Lord, for giving me the capacity to learn from the mistakes of the past, so that I may be more aware of the law of love in the future. May I practise that love in guiding those who follow me through the darkness of their errors to the light of greater understanding that lies beyond.

The Spirit of Truth

> When he comes who is the Spirit of truth, he will
> guide you into all the truth.
>
> John 16.13

This all-important truth-fulfilling property of the Holy Spirit is announced by Jesus in the context of his Farewell Discourses (John 13.33 up to and including chapter 17). He tells his disciples that there is still much that he could say to them, but the burden would be too great for them at that stage. It is the work of the Holy Spirit to continue where he of necessity must come to an end. The Holy Spirit does not speak on his own authority, but only communicates what he hears. He will both make known to them the things that are coming, and give glory to Christ, for everything that he makes known to them he will draw from Christ and therefore from the Father, since all that is the Father's is also Christ's (John 16.12–15).

What does the Holy Spirit hear? Firstly, what is going on in the person's inner life. We may try to separate ourself from the turmoil within us — entertainments on the one hand and furious activity, even for good causes, on the other, are both beguiling ways of escape — but in the end our true situation will be revealed in dreams. If we refuse to pay attention to what these are telling us, the Holy Spirit will bring the lesson home even more definitively in our behaviour and eventually in our state of health.

The Holy Spirit also makes known to us the trend of events in the future; in other words, the creative process is not static, but continues with the life of the universe. Religious faith itself cannot remain static, but is meant to evolve according to the inspiration brought by the Holy Spirit. This does not mean that the basis of faith is mutable; if this were the case any heresy could be passed off as a new revelation of God. What the inspiration of the Holy Spirit brings is a new understanding of God's glory as made evident in the incarnation of his Son Jesus Christ.

A good example of this progressive evolution of spiritual understanding is the emancipation of the slaves. This was not so much as recommended by St Paul when the apostle wrote to Philemon exhorting him to receive his runaway slave Onesimus in charity and forgiveness. That the institution of slavery was wicked was not generally accepted until less than two centuries ago (the Quakers, a group strongly guided by the Holy Spirit, would have no truck with slave-holding earlier on). In the same spirit, we now know that racial, religious and sexist discrimination are intolerable; terrible events in our own time have enlightened even the most stolid members of society.

While this upheaval has proceeded on a spiritual level, the human has steadily come to grips with his environment through inspired scientific research. God who showed his nature as an incarnate being has also revealed the holiness of matter to us, and given us the power to harness it for our own purposes. Whether we proceed beneficially or not depends on our obedience to the inspiration of the Holy Spirit, who leads us to the knowledge of God in Christ when we are humble and actively receptive in contemplative prayer. Jesus himself said, 'Do not suppose that I have come to abolish the Law and the prophets; I did not come to abolish, but to complete' (Matt. 5.17). This is the function of the Holy Spirit, who is to work in all of us.

I like these words:

Our greatest truths are but half-truths. Think not to settle down for ever in any truth, but use it as a tent in which to pass a summer night, but build no house on it, or it will become your tomb. When you first become aware of its insufficiency, and descry some counter-truth looming up in the distance, then weep not, but rejoice: it is the Lord's voice saying, 'Take up your bed and walk'.

The writer was Arthur James Balfour (1848–1930), a politician later to become Prime Minister of Great Britain.

May I ever be so well about your business, Lord, that I do not fail to hear the voice of your Spirit summoning me on to new ventures and fresh fields of service as my accustomed way of thought is rudely jolted by the prompting of the present necessity.

Constancy in Devotion

✧✧

It is only by fidelity in little things that a true and constant love
of God can be distinguished from a passing fervour of spirit.

François Fénelon, *Letters and Reflections*

The moment when we recognize the loved one is indeed glorious.
We are exultant in the radiance of love and can do little else but
offer ourselves unceasingly to its embrace. This applies to human
affection, concentrated in the experience of falling in love with
someone. The joyous abandon seldom lasts long as we see more
clearly into the nature of the beloved — and also into our own need
for clutching on to another person in order to complement our
own psychological inadequacies. There is something faintly
ridiculous about the experience of falling in love when we think
about it later on in the cold light of reason. And yet it remains a
very important component of one's personal growth. ''Tis better to
have loved and lost than never to have loved at all', wrote Alfred
Tennyson in *In Memoriam*. Samuel Butler parodied this well-
known text in *The Way of All Flesh*: ''Tis better to have loved and
lost, than never to have lost at all.' Both sentiments are profoundly
true.

Until one has known the passion of love, one remains enclosed
in oneself. One's life may have been a model of propriety, but the
heart remains cold and uncharitable. Once one has allowed one's
soul to be vulnerable to the attraction of another person, one has
also allowed the greater love of God entrance into one's heart,
which becomes warm and palpitating. The entrance of the Holy
Spirit into one's life allows the imagination to soar into the infinity
of nature, and enormous creative acts of art and generosity become
possible. The tenor of one's normal life may be ludicrously
disrupted, but one has glimpsed the eternal within the temporal
and one's scale of perception will never be as it was before. If this is
so of human affection, it is even more true of the sudden experience
of God's love that brings in its wake a conversion to the light and a
self-giving for the Faith.

The period of intense affection, likened to the honeymoon after marital union, gradually tails away into the humdrum round of daily life. The spouse shows irritating features; likewise, God seems to have forgotten us, and his apparent neglect tries our patience while testing our faith. The test is to proceed onwards, looking less for divine favours and more for strength to proceed in the day's work. It is thus that the reliable, if human and fallible, spouse supports the marriage partner. Likewise the divine providence never fails, provided we play our part in service to God and our fellow creatures. There does come a time, however, when we feel thoroughly let down, our faith is at a low ebb, and we are all for throwing in our hand and quitting on a note of disillusion and even despair. It is now that we prove the authenticity of our original love of the person, or our fervour of commitment to God. Like Job, we may have to lose everything and rail against our fate in unmeasured vehemence, but we must proceed onwards.

What we have to lose is, in fact, our self-centred view of life, that the human beloved and God are here to serve us. Once the ego has been civilized into willing service instead of petulant complaint and childish dominance, we can proceed onwards in equanimity, playing our part day by day in fidelity both to God and our human partner. The love of God is the basis of all that exists, while our love for God is its own reward. In its undemanding embrace we are in heaven now no matter how hard may be the external circumstances. It is in the little things of life that we show our affection most beautifully to those close to us: 'Anything you did for one of my brothers here, however humble, you did for me' (Matt. 25.40).

May I never, Lord, in the exciting thrust of the present attainment, lose sight of the final goal by neglecting the small things of human relationships and of worship.

Purity of Intention

> How blest are those whose hearts are pure;
> they shall see God.

A pure heart has no guile, nor is it soured by malice. It is not disfigured by jealousy, nor is it moved by greed or covetousness. It is empty of all worldly desire, and consequently it is a spacious chamber where God may dwell in peace. Such a heart is found in any young child, at present unsullied by the corruption of the world. Though it is yet uncontaminated by material desires, it is by no means uninhabited: it is the register of the soul, or true self, and responds to the character of the person especially in terms of emotions. It is not a mere void where any and every passing spirit may dwell; on the other hand, it is well guarded by the person against invasion and corruption. But this delectable state of innocence has to be left behind as the person stoops to combat in a society that is geared to material success and personal gain. In other words, the pure heart of the young child is inevitably invaded by mercenary motives and personal desires.

'The heart is the most deceitful of all things, desperately sick; who can fathom it?' (Jer. 17.9). The heart is, above all, the seat of the emotions, and these fluctuate wildly according to our present state of satisfaction. The naked purity of the young heart has to bear with the impress of many cross-currents in the growing life of the person. This experience is a crucial part of our growth to individual maturity; as the heart responds to the stimulus of worldly riches, the temptation to personal power and glory, so it reveals its true calibre. Jesus tells us not to store up for ourselves earthly treasure, which is liable to loss and deterioration, but rather to store up incorruptible heavenly treasure, for where our treasure is, there also will be our heart (Matt. 6.19–20).

The problem with this, and so much other teaching about non-attachment, both in the Sermon on the Mount and in the heights of the other great religious teachings of the world, is its difficulty of attainment. If we believe that a total renunciation of the world's goods is required of us, we soon realize that this is merely a comfortable way of evading personal responsibility for our part in serving the world. Indeed, we have to be more diligent in our labours than ever before, but less centred on our own interests and more on those of the community.

There are a few people whose hearts seem to remain pure as a gift of nature despite all the defilement of the world — perhaps they are saints from birth. But many more of us have to traverse the dark corridors of power and learn the lessons of failure before we can let go of personal desire. Only then do we enter the void where the divine presence welcomes us home. Only when the heart is purified of all craving can we see inwardly to do what is required of us in this transient life. In doing the required work with a clear mind and a pure heart, with single-minded attention and warm compassion, we find that God himself, though always present, is now visible to us.

Jesus told the religious leaders of his time that impressive outer piety is of no avail on its own; it is like cleaning the outside of a cup while leaving the inside dirty. Instead, there must be an inner conversion; if the inside of the cup is cleaned, then the outside will also be spotless (Matt. 23.25–6). Our adult life brings us into close contact with injustice and corruption; the school of suffering helps to purify the heart, which is then in a position to bring the world's darkness to the light. As it does this work, so the heart becomes ever purer and more loving. And so a renewed purity, no longer of childhood innocence but of adult responsibility, is able to accept the world's discord and bring it to a harmony of heavenly peace.

Give me the strength, Lord, to play my part in sharing all the temptations of the world, and the humility to bring them to your presence for acceptance. May the constant awareness of my own impurity be the bond that unites me to my fellows while my cleansing brings greater holiness to them all.

The Proof
of Righteousness

The course of the righteous is like morning light,
growing brighter till it is broad day.

Proverbs 4.18

Those who are righteous are just in their dealings, upright in their response to temptation, virtuous in their behaviour, and law-abiding in their relationships with their fellows and with society as a whole. Righteousness is the peak and end of civilized behaviour. It brings order to a situation that could easily drift into chaos, as it draws light into the dark recesses of the human psyche no less than into the state of affairs of communities and nations.

It is important to distinguish between the righteousness of God and the self-righteousness of inflated people who cannot see beyond the façade they have constructed and the pit of corruption that lies within the psyche. The self-righteous person, typified by the Pharisee in the famous parable of Luke 18.9–14, is so sure of his or her own excellence that there is a constant tendency to look down on other people. In fact, the virtuousness is an imposing front rather than a solid structure, and behind it lies a pit of corruption which looks for rewards and praise to fill it. The truly righteous person is so full of the presence of God that his or her less strong qualities are lit up and exposed to the undemanding love of God, in whom alone healing may be attained.

It is important to recognize the breeding places of impurity and disease that lurk in the body and especially in the psyche of us all. They are conveniently summed up in the 'Seven Deadly Sins': pride, covetousness, lust, anger, gluttony, envy and sloth. It is a useful exercise, at the ending of the day, to check our inventory of deeds against this formidable array, not so much in an attitude of fierce self-accusation as in one of tolerant humour. Most of us are like Peter, James and John with Jesus at Gethsemane: we mean well, but the flesh lets us down. Apart from the obvious sins of the body and mind defined above, there is also the constant temptation

92

to align ourselves to the mode of thinking of our peers, even when we know that we disagree with them but have not the courage to take a firm stand on an important issue. The temptation to let things drift while we choose the quiet life can be far more terrible in its ultimate consequences than any of the conventional deadly sins. I often remember Charles Péguy, a prophetic French Catholic who fought racial and social injustice at the end of the last century and was killed early in the First World War in defence of his country. He wrote, in *Basic Verities*, that the worst of all partialities is to withhold oneself, the worst ignorance is not to act, the worst lie to steal away. He also wrote that the social revolution will be moral, or it will not be. It is hardly surprising that the world still awaits this revolution, despite the many that have been proclaimed in its name.

In other words, our actions have to be balanced against such personal sins as anger, covetousness, envy and lust no matter how passionately we may feel about the causes that animate us. On the other hand, we should not let tolerance and discretion slide insidiously into sloth. Nor should we be so sure of our own rectitude that we cannot receive adverse criticism; otherwise pride, the cardinal sin, will take root and certainly lead us to destruction. And the senses should always be controlled by the spirit, lest their undisciplined satisfaction end in a gluttony that obliterates all finer feelings and leads to bodily and mental disease.

When we have our own house in order, we can see and respond to the divine light which encompasses all creation. And then our passage through life illuminates the way of those who follow, as they glorify God (Matt. 5.16).

Give me, Lord, the wisdom to see my failings, the humility to work towards their healing, and the courage to stand out for what I believe to be true, even when all human support is withdrawn and I have only the silence as friend.

True Sacrifice

> The offerings of the righteous are the tears of their eyes, and
> a sacrifice pleasing to God is their sighings during vigil.
>
> St Isaac of Syria, *Directions on Spiritual Training*, 206

A theme that pervades much of the prophetic literature of the Old
Testament is the priority of moral decency over ritual sacrifice.
When we read the ritual requirements of the Mosaic law, we are
spontaneously revolted by the shedding of animal blood and the
sacrifice of animal flesh to appease a ferocious tribal God. Yet even
in this primitive ritual there is the concept of something valuable
being dedicated to the Creator, so that the owner is relatively
impoverished.

But it becomes all too easy to use material objects as a substitute
for inner dedication. As the ancient rabbis knew, God wants the
heart. If our earthly gifts are offered in a spirit of genuine devotion,
they are pleasing to the Deity, but if they are used as a sort of
smoke-screen to hide our basic indifference to holy living, they are
thrust back at us in disgust. The smoke-screen does not deceive
God, but it can easily create in us a sense of false sanctity. And so a
sacrifice wrongly presented can be on the one hand a focus of
superstition and on the other a blanket of complacency. The object
of sacrifice is made holy by being given to God in love; where this
element of self-giving is absent, the gift is a lifeless thing. And so
Hosea wrote:

> Loyalty is my desire, not sacrifice,
> not whole-offerings but the knowledge of God. (Hos. 6.6)

We have to learn, progressively in the school of life, that we
ourselves can alone provide a gift to God that is holy, that can in
turn renew the lives of those around us. These include, in the final
judgement, all that is created by God.

The supreme sacrifice, in Christian understanding, is the self-
giving death of Jesus on the cross. He atones for the collective sin
of humanity by reconciling a vicious world to divine love, which

now flows out in pure grace to all who will receive it. Through the influence of the Risen Lord, whose body is now one with the eternal light of God, humanity itself is brought to that light in preparation for its own transfiguration. And so the words of Psalm 51.17 become intensely real:

My sacrifice, O God, is a broken spirit;
a wounded heart, O God, thou wilt not despise.

It is only then that material sacrifice attains reality, whether of animals as in the Psalmist's time (Ps. 51.19), or of money and other possessions later on. Here we can remember the widow's mite at the Temple treasury, which was preferred by Jesus to the much larger donations of the wealthy worshippers: she gave of herself, while the others gave merely of their excess (Mark 12.41-4).

With these thoughts we can proceed to St Isaac's emphasis on contrition being a nobler sacrifice to God than anything on a more material level. When the righteous cry, they give of their very essence to God, even the sins which would usually be concealed from their closest brethren. It is a thought that even the greatest gift we may offer God — and all gifts come from him to us, who are then expected to use them and bring back something beautiful to him from our labours and sufferings — is as nothing compared with the gift of ourselves, even soiled and revolting in the world's eyes. This is the measure of love, the supreme gift of God and our full sacrifice to our fellows and the world. It is this that we offer our Lord at the end of the day as we proceed to fall, like little children, into a sleep of oblivion that carries us forward for the encounters of the next day.

Even when we are soiled and dispirited, we at least prove that we have shared in the world's strife, even if not especially creditably. The righteous are not some remote spiritual élite who grace the world by their presence; we are they when we give our uncleanness to God in simple faith.

May I have the honesty, Lord, to face my sinfulness, the humility to offer it to you as my sacrifice, and the faith to proceed even when little outward change appears to bless my life. Instead, may I give of myself unceasingly to the less fortunate members of the community.

SIX

Grace and Free Will

Seeking God

Comfort yourself, you would not seek me if you had not found me.

Blaise Pascal, *Pensées*, 3.553

Is there a purpose behind the apparently random events in any life? Does meaning play any part in our existence, or do we simply delude ourselves when we are able to discern a pattern behind seemingly fortuitous occurrences in our daily lives? Does God exist, and if so what sort of a being stands there before a universe in black disorder? The human has pondered these questions since the dawn of his peculiar intelligence. Various religious geniuses have emerged, each having some glimpse of the reality that appears to lie behind the treadmill of endless human activity. The philosophical or spiritual systems they have pioneered invariably tend to become rigid and imprisoning in the hands of their disciples. We all want assurance, and those in charge of the tradition look also for power, allegedly to spread the doctrine but more subtly to gain ascendance over their peers.

In the world of science truth can be contrasted sharply from falsehood, the deciding factors being logic on the one hand and experiment that can be repeated on the other. When we enter the more diffuse world of values the contrast between truth and falsehood, beauty and ugliness, goodness and evil is equally sharp, but the criteria are inner, personal ones. We learn to make our own decisions, since the opinions of our friends and neighbours vary to the point of total discordance. The existence of a number of higher religions, each with its own complement of saints, teaches us that spiritual truth is far more embracing than the fundamentalist would have us believe. Anyone who sets out to prove the superiority of a particularly spiritual tradition or way of life over its rivals shows in the end only his or her own mental constitution and the nature of the prejudices governing it. On the whole, the young are very assured about the basic issues of life; increasing age, with the experience that accrues from the various events and encounters that have attended it, makes us less certain but very much wiser.

The somewhat dogmatic God of organized religion drops into the background as we discover the living God in whom we all live and move and have our existence (Acts 17.28).

Whenever we are moved by a noble action, a beautiful piece of art or music, or the dedication of a person who will not let rest enter his or her life before a particular work of goodness is carried out, we know the unknown God who is closer to us than our own identity. Can natural beauty also reveal its Creator to us? Indeed it can: if we cannot see the work of God in the world of tangible phenomena, we are not likely to discover him in non-material realms. This is the deeper meaning of incarnation, and stresses the importance of corporeal existence in the development of the human personality. Nevertheless, there is something even greater in human art: natural beauty has been ennobled by human toil and the suffering that is part of meaningful existence.

We know God within ourselves; without that inner knowledge we would not seek the beautiful, the honest and the good, which shows itself fully in unreserved sacrificial love. Whenever we are raised in consciousness from the self-centred life of the world to the self-giving life of compassion we have found the divine principle within us. We seek to make intelligible and therefore articulate what is deeply set in our soul. But God cannot be so manipulated. As Dietrich Bonhoeffer said in *No Rusty Swords*, 'A God who let us prove his existence would be an idol.' He also said, even more challengingly, 'The only way to be honest is to recognize that we have to live in the world even if God is not there' (*Letters and Papers from Prison*). It is in that frame of mind, in fact, that we know him within us.

May I never lose the courage of my own convictions about your presence in my life, Lord, even when the edifice of my world lies shattered about my feet. Then may I continue onwards, trusting in my own integrity.

The Will of God

In his will is our peace.

Dante Alighieri, *The Divine Comedy: Paradise*

Indeed, to know the will of God in our little lives is what the spiritual aspirant in us wants most of all. Then we could relax, trusting God to show us the right way while we simply followed his directions, rather like a computer programmed for a specific piece of work.

But how can we discover the divine will? The more desperately we search, the more surely does the cloud of frustration envelop us. If we are unwise enough to consult other people renowned for their gift of discernment, whether of a natural psychic disposition or a more definitely Christian charismatic commitment, we are very liable to place ourselves under their domination; and human nature being what it is, the person will all too easily accept the open invitation to control our life according to some inner directive. None of us is free from prejudice, which in turn cannot but cloud our judgement even if we sincerely offer ourself to the service of God and our fellows.

It is strange in this respect to reflect on Jeremiah's promise: 'If you search with all your heart, I will let you find me, says the Lord' (Jer. 29.13). The emphasis here is on the heart: Dietrich Bonhoeffer (in *Letters and Papers from Prison*) said that the 'heart' in the biblical sense is not the inward life, but the whole person in relation to God. Therefore in terms of our quest for the divine will, we can only begin to realize it when we are prepared to offer our whole being to God, not merely an egoistical grasping for God's support. If we seek God with only a part of us, he eludes our grasp, but if we are prepared to offer our very being to the quest, even though our body may perish in the enterprise, our deeper consciousness of reality, which we call the soul, will touch the divine ground, and we will know eternal life. Admittedly this knowledge starts in hazy shafts, but as the life of the spirit proceeds and we are divested of outer possessions (these are the idols so constantly attacked by the prophets of Israel), so we come into a much more constant relationship with God.

The sincerity of our quest is measured by the devotion we show to the common round of existence which we encounter day by day. Like Martha, we are to find the divine presence in the routine tasks that confront us, no matter how uninspiring our work may be. Therefore the will of God is to be found in our present situation, our 'sacrament of the present moment' as Jean-Pierre de Caussade calls it in his spiritual classic *Self-Abandonment to Divine Providence*. To work as efficiently as possible and as harmoniously as we can with the people around us is what God wants of us at any one time and place. If we do our apportioned task satisfactorily, greater work will lie ahead of us: the Parable of the Talents (Matt. 25.14–30) is our guide here. A time may well come when an inner prompting, coming quite spontaneously either during prayer or simply in the course of our daily routine, will inform us that something more is required of us. This is the type of vocation that moves one to dedicate one's life to ministry or religious vows, but often it is less spectacular than this, and simply calls one to a more committed work in the world under Christian allegiance. Our Lord is present where even two or three are met together in his name (Matt. 18.20). And where he is, his will inspires all our efforts.

When he calls us, showing us his will, he is much more likely to come to us directly than through the mediation of a third party. We are therefore well advised to look warily at all unsought, proffered advice that comes to us from someone claiming special inspiration. If we cannot discern the movement of the Holy Spirit within us, we are unlikely to know its truth in anyone else.

May I have, Lord, such inner peace of mind that I can be about your business at all times, confident that I am doing your will, but always open to new directions of service appropriate to changed situations of times and places.

Inner Renewal

✧✧✧✧✧✧✧✧✧✧✧✧✧✧✧✧✧✧✧✧✧✧✧ ✧✧✧✧✧✧✧✧✧✧✧✧✧✧✧✧✧✧✧✧✧✧✧✧✧✧✧✧✧

> Though our outward humanity is in decay, yet day by day
> we are inwardly renewed.
>
> 2 Corinthians 4.16

We can hardly avoid identifying the whole of ourselves with our present situation and the pattern of our preceding existence. When we look back dispassionately upon our past life, with all its vows and promises unfulfilled or broken, we remember with irony the familiar doxology, 'As it was in the beginning, is now, and shall be for ever. Amen.' Must we always be falling into the pit of lust, gluttony or covetousness? Can we never stop repeating unsavoury gossip and making subtle mischief against our neighbours and even those whom we regard as colleagues and friends?

Jeremiah in one of his most passionate outbursts cries out:

> The heart is the most deceitful of all things,
> desperately sick; who can fathom it? (17.9)

and again:

> Can the Nubian change his skin,
>   or the leopard his spots?
> And you? Can you do good,
>   you who are schooled in evil? (13.23)

And yet, despite the constant recrimination of a conscience that refuses to be totally overridden by the current mode of mass deception which strives to justify the mean and shoddy and sneers at any ideal of perfection, there is an inner core, a spark in the centre of that conscience, that will never cease from driving us on to the goal of self-fulfilment. This is not to be equated with material success, which at its highest is transient as the shades of retirement and ageing cloud all human ambitions. Indeed, we can never in this life know whether we are truly fulfilled as people. But Jesus gives us the key in the Sermon on the Mount: 'There must be no limit to your goodness, as your heavenly Father's goodness knows no bounds' (Matt. 5.48). The spark of the soul where the conscience finds its most radiant expression knows the measure of that goodness, and will never rest until that challenge of perfection has been met and its end attained.

When, at the ending of the day, we most bitterly bewail our shortcomings, feeling that we never seem to make any improvement and that there is no moral or spiritual soundness in us, there is a power within us whose origin is divine, working unceasingly to supplant the past inadequacies with a new vigour of enterprise and a greater sensitivity of purpose. This is the grace, the unmerited gift, of God working a slow change in our inner attitudes, so that, according to our own willingness to receive the gift of love, our old ways are slowly erased and a fresh perspective of existence shows itself in our lives. To be sure, we can do nothing of ourselves, but God working within us can replace what was immature and selfish with a character of deepening responsibility and caring for others. It is during the time of sleep, when we yield our being to the divine in trusting obedience and quiet content, that this slow renewal takes effect. Of course, in one respect the change is continuous, but in another it shows itself most impressively after the hush of sleep has obliterated the usual self-concern that can so easily interpose itself between the action of God and the benefit of the individual.

To regret an inadequate attitude of the past is to set in motion the decay of our outward humanity; to wait in humility for the action of God in the soul is the first step in our inward renewal. The regret cancels out our previous pride that will not accept God's grace; the humility is the foundation stone on which the new person is being fashioned. But then we have to play our part in substantiating the inward renewal to the point of creating a new person of a pattern shown us in the life of Jesus himself.

O Lord, may I cease to cling on to outworn attitudes of mind, and be always open to the thrust of your Spirit, guiding me into new paths of endeavour which heighten my awareness to the feelings and requirements of my fellow creatures.

Being about
our Father's Business

❖❖❖❖❖❖❖❖❖❖❖❖❖❖❖❖❖❖❖ ❖❖❖❖❖❖❖❖❖❖❖❖❖❖❖❖❖❖❖❖❖❖❖❖

> While daylight lasts we must carry on the work of him
> who sent me; night comes, when no one can work.

John 9.4

Jesus makes this urgent admonition as he performs the miracle of
giving sight to a man blind from birth. It reminds us also of the
comparatively short time at our disposal during the active years of
our life, and how important it is to act now. The seventh deadly
sin, sloth, is the most insidious of them all, for there are usually so
many good reasons why we should delay doing what ought to be
done while we slink away with guilt into the shadows, where we
hope we will avoid detection while the trouble quietly evaporates.

On the other hand, immediate action can easily assume an
obsessional character, so that we feel we must always show the flag
and be unceasingly involved in every social or ecclesiastical issue in
order to attest to our Christian commitment. Activism is also an
insidious evil in the spiritual life: we become so involved in social
or other matters that God is eased out of the picture; while his
influence is always with us when we attempt to do our basic duties,
we may become too busy to set aside time in which to hear without
distraction the divine voice speaking within us. It is one thing to be
inspired to a nobler calling, but quite another to hear inwardly how
best to proceed. So much confusion is caused by the type of
individual who means well but simply gets in the way of others
who are better qualified to deal with the matter.

Therefore the first work we all should heed in the daylight hours
of active, youthful endeavour is that of drawing closer to God in
wordless contemplation. Such an activity can also be followed
when the night of illness or old age casts its shadow on the routine
of our lives, drawing us up with a jolt to consider the facts of
mundane existence. But, interestingly enough, it is easier to pray
silently to God when one is in the throes of turmoil than when one

is relaxed on holiday or completely retired from work. Active participation in the world's show seems a necessary stimulus for effective prayer. On the other hand, a remoteness from the world's problems seems to make us more distant from our Creator. Prayer therefore loses something of its urgency as it becomes increasingly an attitude of general good will without the bite of personal commitment.

Immediately following the quotation from St John's Gospel above, Jesus speaks about carrying on God's work which is to bring light to the world: 'While I am in the world I am the light of the world' (John 9.5). This is the work of all of us, and the deeper implication of the miracle is that Christ is here to give sight to all who will receive. As so often happens, those who are full of their own rectitude wilfully remain blind to higher spiritual truth, whereas the humble and suffering people can grasp the gift of vision. Thus the congenitally blind man received spiritual as well as physical sight, while the hostile group of Pharisees blinded themselves further in rejecting the one who came with healing gifts to bestow on them also.

Our task here on earth is also to bring the light of God's love to all whom we meet in our day's work. Whether our work is considered menial or exalted by the world's standards is of little importance; what matters is the dedication of our efforts and the love we bring to others on the way. In the stern commission of St Teresa of Avila to her Carmelite community, we too have our marching orders: 'Remember, Christ has no body now on earth but yours, no hands but yours, no feet but yours; yours are the eyes through which is to look out Christ's compassion to the world; yours are the feet with which he is to go about doing good; and yours are the hands with which he is to bless us now.'

May I always have such dedication to the world, Lord, that I may be about your business when tempted by the diversion of the passing scene to cease my labour and rest in idleness. May I also remember to rest in your refreshing peace before I move onward, so that I may bring that peace to the world.

Little Acts of Kindness

****

That best portion of a good man's life,
His little, nameless, unremembered acts
of kindness and of love.

William Wordsworth, 'Lines composed a few miles above Tintern Abbey'

As we enter more deeply into our own inner being, especially when
we prepare to retire to bed, we are well advised to reflect
dispassionately on the course of the day's work, both on the
outstanding events and on our emotional reactions to their
challenge. What we desire most is comfort and security, for then
our equilibrium remains undisturbed and we can enjoy the present
moment without forebodings of trouble. But life does not deal so
considerately with us: we are continually being jolted out of our rut
of easy satisfaction by circumstances that alternatively irritate,
anger or frighten us. It is our full response to these incursions into
our peace of mind that is the measure of our spiritual condition.

When we are called on to help a friend at the cost of our own
convenience, do we, like the householder described in Luke 11.5-8,
respond harshly and ungraciously, or do we give of our time and
resources unstintingly? If we have indeed shown an uncharitable
strain, we do well to recollect the matter and give our apologies to
God. One hopes that, as in that parable, one did relent in time, so
that a cordial relationship was maintained with the other person. If
one's recalcitrance persisted, the confession to God should be
followed as soon as possible by an apology to one's neighbour.
However, not all recollections need have a dark, negative face.
There are occasions in a day's toil when one may be agreeably
surprised by one's charity, a spontaneous outpouring of caring to
someone in distress, quite probably a complete stranger who then
passes on his or her way as if there had been no encounter.

The practice of meditating on major events in a day's life before
one goes to bed is strongly to be recommended. How one has
behaved is an excellent indication of one's state of spiritual health.
What is called for is not a period of morbid introspection in which

106

the state of one's soul is pondered upon in humourless intensity, but rather a reflection on the sum of the day's achievements and experiences, with a comment on one's reaction to the test.

We tend quite often to denigrate ourselves, comparing ourselves unfavourably with some other person or even with an acknowledged saint. And yet we know little of the inner life of those whom we especially admire. St Teresa of Avila prayed, 'God deliver us from sullen saints.' It is not the virtuousness of a person that necessarily testifies to his or her spiritual excellence. Many of Jesus' parables and encounters in real life appear to prefer the acknowledged sinner who confesses his or her fault to their cold, clean-living detractors who sadly lack any spark of common humanity. This may indeed have been extinguished by their obsessional striving for inner purity to the detriment of warm, accommodating compassion.

And so it is our humble, scarcely remembered acts of kindness, especially when we were hard pressed with little time to spare amid our busy schedule, that are the best part of our lives. By these we will be remembered, not so much by a grateful person thanking us effusively for our good offices, but by many toilers on the way whose travail we have spontaneously lightened by our courtesy and consideration, when they were in the darkness of death and completely disillusioned about human kindness.

I thank you, Lord, for the pattern of generous living which you have provided in the witness of the many people around me who have supported me by their innate kindness. May my own heart so expand in compassion that I too can bring the rays of your love to my fellows in the course of my work during the remainder of my life on earth.

The Joy of
Honest Achievement

❖❖❖❖❖❖❖❖❖❖❖❖❖❖❖❖❖❖❖❖❖ ❖❖❖❖❖❖❖❖❖❖❖❖❖❖❖❖❖❖❖❖❖❖❖❖❖

Whatever you are doing, put your whole heart into it,
as if you were doing it for the Lord and not for men.

Colossians 3.23

We tend, in our ignorance of true merit, to classify actions
according to their material fruit, which in turn is judged by the
amount of money they earn or the degree of power they engender.
In this frame of mind we would exalt the work of a doctor tending
the sick, a lawyer investigating the intricate processes of litigation
on behalf of his or her client, or a politician wrestling with great
affairs of state, above that of a cleaner or a simple artisan in the
employ of a large, rather impersonal firm. Even if we were
considering a single action graded in excellence of execution, it
would appear quite obvious that the star performer was achieving
results of quite a different calibre to the mere amateur. In the end
the less gifted artist or athlete might be tempted to lose heart and
throw in her hand, realizing the futility of competing with such
excellence. And so a great deal of wholesome enjoyment might be
lost through envy and self-denigration.

In practice, this extreme reaction is uncommon. We all have to
earn our living, and if providence decrees that only less exalted
work is left for us, we soon learn to be grateful for this small
mercy; at least it keeps us from destitution, especially in times of
mass unemployment. In a rather similar state of mind, we find that
exercising our modest artistic or athletic talents is quite satisfying
in its own right, and as we proceed so we lose the inhibiting self-
consciousness that prevents us fulfilling our own potential. But
even greater satisfaction will come to us if we do the action in real
gratitude for the One who made that work possible. We begin to
learn that all work done for him is its own blessing, no matter what
valuation is put upon it by the outside world. A room cleaned with
devotion so as to make it pleasant for work or recreation brings

with it more than mere order and freshness; it brings the personality of the cleaner with it, and by the devoted toil, a blessing fills the space. A meal prepared with love has a very different savour from one that is hastily put together as mere drudgery, a thought that brings us back to poor Martha preparing the repast for Jesus but with so much annoyance in her heart.

It is far better to perform a menial work with devotion than a high-powered one with indifference. Nowadays much routine work can be delegated to computers which are, if anything, even more accurate than humans in their particular programmes. But it is the person who presents the result to the client that makes the essential relationship and fulfils the real contract. We have to see that the work is its own blessing or curse according to our personal attitude. While some professions demand expert skills and are therefore justly more highly regarded, the end result is the same: the satisfaction of the customer. To have attained this requirement in integrity is all that is asked of us. If we do well in small things, greater ones will come our way, because concern has warmed our efficiency.

In the quotation above we are enjoined to do our work as for God, but if we perform it in concern for our neighbour we are serving God at the same time. As Tertullian wrote: 'When thou seest thy brother, thou seest thy Lord.' The reward for the service is a greater knowledge of God. St Francis de Sales wrote, in *Of the Love of God*, that great works do not always lie in our way, but every minute we may do little ones excellently, that is, with great love.

I thank you, Lord, that I can do so many small things to keep alive and play my part in serving the community. May my eyes be fixed on what is attainable for me personally rather than on the exploits of those whose gifts are quite different from mine. May the small and the great, the feeble and the exalted, share what they have for the benefit of the whole community.

Blissful Sleep

❖❖❖❖❖❖❖❖❖❖❖❖❖❖❖❖❖❖❖❖ ❖❖❖❖❖❖❖❖❖❖❖❖❖❖❖❖❖❖❖❖❖❖❖❖

Sweet is the sleep of the labourer . . .

Ecclesiastes 5.12

Charles Péguy wrote, in *Basic Verities*, a marvellous poem about sleep:

> Sleep is the friend of man.
> Sleep is the friend of God.
> Sleep is perhaps the most beautiful thing I have created.
> I myself rested on the seventh day.
> He whose heart is pure, sleeps
> And he who sleeps has a pure heart.

In the quotation from Ecclesiastes the text continues, '. . . whether he eats little or much; but the rich man owns too much and cannot sleep.' This is the heart of the matter: when one is filled with cares, it is difficult to let go of oneself sufficiently for God's great gift of sleep to wash away the inner litter, and prepare a table so clean that the Eucharistic vessels may be set in place for us to eat at the heavenly banquet in the presence of our Lord. When we are full of the emptiness of simplicity, God can enter and bless our mind and body in the sleep of heaven, and so renew our full being for the heavy work ahead of us. For our work is heavy, even if we have little outwardly to do: we are to bear the inner burdens of those around us. As St Paul says, in Galatians 6.2: 'Help one another to carry these heavy loads, and in this way you will fulfil the law of Christ.'

In the poem of Péguy quoted above, I have purposely omitted the preceding line — 'I don't like the man who doesn't sleep, says God' — because insomnia need not be a consequence of moral deficiency. It is not infrequently a symptom of clinical depression, and often accompanies states of morbid anxiety. Indeed, God, who I believe wants us all to be healed of our infirmities, surely does not like the agony of sleeplessness; but I cannot imagine his deep love being withdrawn from any of his creatures, even when they are much too busy with worldly schemes to spare a thought of gratitude for their Creator.

The secret of falling asleep, like so many other activities, is to let go, quite consciously falling into the sustaining arms of God. Sleep comes as a peak of untroubled faith; it is the point where trust in God is proved in the work of acceptance. None of us knows what will happen during the period of oblivion that follows, but we submit in joyful acceptance, just as we did when we were little children. The person with the burden of many possessions has greater difficulty in letting them go, as we all shall when we know that greatest sleep which we call death. And I am confident that then also we shall awake even more refreshed than during earthly life to share in God's heavenly banquet, before we are sent on to do the work ahead of us, which is to bring the day of God's glory closer to our world, and through it to the entire universe.

Shelley wrote, 'How wonderful is Death, Death and his brother Sleep!' (in both 'The Daemon of the World' and 'Queen Mab'). It is not inappropriate to end with some more Péguy:

Nothing is so beautiful as a child going to sleep while he is
    saying his prayers, says God.
I tell you nothing is so beautiful in the world —
And getting his *Our Father* mixed up with his *Hail, Mary.*
Nothing is so beautiful and it is even one point
on which the Blessed Virgin agrees with me —
And I can say it is the only point on which we agree.
Because as a rule we disagree,
She being for mercy,
Whereas I, of course, have to be for justice.

I thank you, Lord, for your beautiful gift of sleep. I pray that my life may be so dedicated to your glory and the service of my brothers that I may bring them that love that finds its proof in tranquil sleep.

111

The Peace of God

❖❖❖❖❖❖❖❖❖❖❖❖❖❖❖❖❖❖❖❖ ❖❖❖❖❖❖❖❖❖❖❖❖❖❖❖❖❖❖❖❖❖❖❖❖❖❖❖❖❖❖

> Thou dost keep in peace men of constant mind,
> in peace because they trust in thee.
>
> Isaiah 26.3

An earlier translation of this verse in the Authorized Version of
the Bible is: 'Thou wilt keep him in perfect peace, whose mind is
stayed on thee: because he trusteth in thee.' The value of this
translation lies not only in its greater power of expression, a tribute
to the beauty of the language of an age long past, but even more
pertinently in its juxtaposition of constancy of mind with
contemplation of the divine reality, so that the person's attention
never falls away from God no matter how far his or her concern
may appear to diverge from religious matters. Constancy of mind is
a state in which we are completely attentive to the demands of the
present moment. There is a clarity of awareness that precludes all
extraneous thoughts, all adverse emotions and all purposeless
actions. This does not mean that thought, emotion and action are
simply abolished so that we enter into a state of impassive trance. It
means rather that all psychological and psychic energies are directed
in dedicated awareness to God, even if the divine presence is not
directly recognized.

St Paul, in Philippians 4.8, gives an essential clue: 'And now,
my friends, all that is true, all that is noble, all that is just and pure,
all that is lovable and gracious, whatever is excellent and admirable
— fill all your thoughts with these things.' As our minds are filled
with elements of beauty, truth and goodness, so the less admirable
and more destructive thoughts and emotions, both from within
ourselves and from the outside environment of human malice and
fear, are quietly eased out of our lives. This is not crude 'positive
thinking' in which the less pleasant aspects of life are ignored and
stifled by good thoughts that refuse to face the fact of evil and
suffering. It is simply a condition of full self-giving to the present
situation, with an awareness unclouded by negative thoughts and
emotions that would pre-empt any possible good result even before
the work was started.

In a state of constancy of mind all prejudices are transcended, and we are in direct communication with the source of all life, the Holy Spirit. This Spirit cleanses our emotions and ennobles our minds so that a warm love can flow through us and from us to the surrounding world. In this way the darkness of existence is quietly accepted and then lifted up to God for a blessing. Its negative emotional charge is so neutralized that it too can share in the divine radiance. One cannot be constantly aware of the present moment until one can trust God, otherwise one's mind will be continually roving around in disquietude. Once we are so constantly aware we are, in fact, rooted in God's presence. Conversely, 'the practice of the presence of God' (the title of a lovely little book by Brother Lawrence) brings us to the requirements of immediate action, which we can then perform in an attitude of trust. This trust brings with it a peace beyond human reckoning: it is a state of union with God and with our fellow creatures in which there is the bliss of complete trust and unconditional acceptance.

When I know I am nothing in the world's eyes, I can identify myself with everything: nothing human, indeed no creature, is foreign to me. God is the supreme No-Thing, for no mortal concept can define, let alone contain, him. The constant mind is so transparent that it leaves us open to see and accept all that exists. This is true freedom: 'poor ourselves, we bring wealth to many; penniless, we own the world' (2 Cor. 6.10). Indeed, though we have nothing for our own, yet we possess all things, for at last we can truly enjoy the gifts of God without wanting to appropriate them for our own support.

Teach me, Lord, so to trust the beneficence of life that even when encompassed by a sea of troubles, I can face the future with a clear mind, sufficient to do what is required of me as a responsible adult fashioned in your own likeness.

Peace of Heart

How blest are the peacemakers;
God shall call them his sons.

Matthew 5.9

In its full glory, peace is attained when there is such openness
between us and God that we can share his presence with trust, and
bring that presence with us to all whom we may meet in the course
of the day's work. In this sharing we can enjoy the good things that
God has given us, but which we usually guard lest they be disfigured
by our fellows or even removed by their malicious action. In fact,
we cannot fully enjoy anything until it can be shared with other
people; when we are secure in the knowledge of God we can share
without reservation, knowing that nothing belongs exclusively to
anyone in perpetuity but that each may have the privilege of
stewardship of a particular gift for a certain period of time before it
is inevitably relinquished to those who follow on.

How can we know that peace which the world cannot give, but
which Jesus promised to his disciples, so that their troubled hearts
might be set at rest and their fears banished (John 14.27)? The
answer is simple: be open to the divine presence at all times, even,
and especially, when you are in trouble. I would not go as far as
some people who actually thank God for adversity, since this has
masochistic overtones, but we can remember St Paul's view that all
things work together for good for those who love God (Rom.
8.28). We remember in this context that Jesus himself, who is
called the peace that brought together Gentile and Jew (Eph.
2.14), nevertheless warned his disciples that he had not come to
bring peace, but a sword, for with his advent there would be strife
between members of individual families (Matt. 10.34–5), to say
nothing of the larger world which was rocked by the uncom-
promising demands made by him in his teaching and in the style of
living he represented. In this he was preceded by the prophets of
the Old Testament, notably Jeremiah, who castigated the false

114

prophets of peace when there was no decency and loyalty to God in the hearts of the people.

Peacemaking is evidently something more than simply juggling with present circumstances so as to placate as many people as possible. It is rather the capacity to warm people's hearts and enlighten their minds so that they can see the greater prospect of life that shines beyond the present difficulties. In the Old Testament this was prophesied to be the work of Elijah: to reconcile families before the terrible day of the Lord (Mal. 4.5–6). Jesus identified the returned Elijah with John the Baptist (Matt. 11.15).

To bring peace to others, we must first be at peace with ourselves, accepting our full complement of characteristics, the adverse no less than those which we regard as favourable. Then we can be the instrument of peace to those around us, as well as those more distant, through the medium of prayer. When we are at peace within ourselves, we quite spontaneously flow out in compassion to others, while the Holy Spirit puts words in our mouths and actions in our limbs that bring relief to all who are in trouble. Each night, as we prepare for bed, let us open ourselves to God's mercy by acknowledging our feelings of aversion and intolerance, and giving them to God as our urgent sacrifice. He will lift them from us provided we pray for those whom we heartily dislike, at the same time asking that our own hardness of heart may be healed. In the daytime let us put a seal on our lips, so that we do not blurt out our unguarded opinions about other people before we have had time to reflect. And when harsh judgements fill us with self-righteousness, let us call on God for his mercy on our own acts of thoughtlessness and words of unkindness. As we change in character, so we bring peace to others, who likewise undergo changes from darkness to light. And so we may all approach more fully to divine sonship.

May your blessing of peace, Lord, so inspire me that I move from self-centred concern to a warm regard for all creatures, knowing that peace comes only with unconditional giving of myself to all around me.

SEVEN

The Universal Hope

The Inner Christ

> Do not try to discriminate the worthy from the unworthy,
> but let all people be equal in your eyes for a good deed.

St Isaac of Syria, *Directions on Spiritual Training*, 172

It may seem rather strange to us, who live in a pluralistic, decidedly permissive society, that there should be any discrimination of people according to their worthiness, especially after they have done something good. Surely a good deed confers worthiness on the person who has done it, whatever his or her background may be! Nevertheless, there is a snob in most of us, not so much today perhaps on the social level, but more decidedly on the spiritual path.

Fundamentalist groups can hardly avoid believing that only those who follow a strict faith according to a written scripture and tradition can be saved. There is certainly enough in the New Testament to affirm this point of view. St Peter, for instance, in the course of his evangelistic address to his fellow Jews which was occasioned by the miraculous healing of a man crippled from birth, stated that, apart from Jesus, there is no salvation in anyone else at all, for there is no other name under heaven granted to us, by which we may receive salvation (Acts 4.12). A similar sort of dogmatic exclusiveness is apparently contained in John 14.6: 'I am the way; I am the truth and I am the life; no one comes to the Father except by me.' Claims of strident arrogance can also be found in the ranks of fervent Jewish and Muslim believers; except, of course, that the object of their emphatic faith is not Jesus but a particular tenet of their own tradition. This variation in the means of salvation can hardly escape the amused notice of the agnostic; when one considers the cruelty done in the name of sectarian religion, one can be excused for saying, in the slightly altered words of Shakespeare, 'A plague on all your houses'.

In the end, the matter is brought into rational perspective not so much by any belief system of people as by the innate nobility that lies deep, often dormant, in the human soul. So often it is overlaid by selfish, even violent, impulses, but then it is suddenly ignited by the Holy Spirit, and the awakened person sees clearly and does the right thing. The charitable concern of the Good Samaritan who went at once to help a fellow human in distress is an unforgettable example. When a committed Christian witnesses such a good deed, he or she should sound a long prayer of praise to God, from whom all good things come. The Lord has shown himself in the person, and a new way of life is being opened to both the benefactor and the observer (this includes the object of assistance and also the bystander who witnesses the noble action). Whether the benefactor subscribes to a particular religion or not, whatever the political affiliations or life-style, the inner Christ has been revealed in him or her. The name of the presence may not be known to the person who has done well, but his transforming power will never cease in its renewing work so long as he is welcomed within. The way and life of Jesus show the truth.

It is here that the Christian may help. St Isaac of Syria continues: 'For in this way you can attract even the unworthy towards God, since the soul is easily led to the fear of God by means of bodily things.' No matter how perverse the character of the one who has done a good deed (one thinks of the prostitutes and tax-gatherers in the ministry of Jesus), once that person has been affirmed as a fellow human being on the road to God, the light will shine ever more brightly in the soul and the tendency towards indecency and selfishness will wane. The awe (a more helpful understanding than naked fear) of God in his or her own being will move the person ever onwards towards completion.

A last thought: our attitude to people moulds their personality to conform with our prejudices; thus do unfriendly national, racial and religious stereotypes arise. Let us think kindly of people, forgetting their origin and mode of life, and seeing them as unique creatures of God.

I thank you, Lord, for the tendency to kindness and compassion you have planted within me. May I so conduct my own life that I evoke similar considerate behaviour in my fellow human beings.

Parts of the One Body

What will God say to us, if some of us go to him without the others?

Charles Péguy

What we are ultimately to become is an issue that lies at the heart of the process of creation. It impinges upon our thoughts as we retire for rest. There is first the matter of our own end in terms of the life we have lived here. But above this rather self-centred approach there is the matter of creation itself, remembering that each of us is a part of the whole. The contribution we make may not be especially startling in worldly terms, but our psychical emanation may affect the lives of the many who work alongside us, for good or for bad. In the famous words of John Donne, 'No man is an island entire of itself — any man's death diminishes me, because I am involved in mankind; and therefore never send to know for whom the bell tolls; it tolls for thee.' Yes, indeed, we are all part of a greater continent, and the whole is not complete until each part is healthy and so functioning to its full capacity, true to itself, that it can make its own unique contribution to the whole.

In this respect the whole is greater than the sum of its parts, for the glow of individual contributions is expanded into a glorious radiance far in excess of the sum of the total participation when people work together in a unison of intent to praise their Creator and serve the common good. It is hard for the untried person to envisage any good that transcends personal grandeur of the type that wealth or power may provide. It may require a radical stripping of all earthly supports before the inner integrity is glimpsed and then slowly attained: the account of the Prodigal Son is the classical example. When we are nothing in the world's eyes — and also in our own eyes — we may be much closer to God than even during our time of material splendour and religious certitude: the progress of Job guides us here. We come to God as naked as did Adam and Eve before their momentous fall. After it their nakedness separated them from God, but not he from them. Only when we regain the beautiful simplicity of pure nakedness can we go to him again, and

120

then, to our amazement, we find that we are accompanied by many other naked people, clothed only in the purity of restored innocence.

In this state of being there is no trace of triumphalistic assurance such as we may see in the type of revivalist who parades personal salvation before the world, exhorting everyone to repent and acknowledge God according to a theological formula before it is too late: or else the alternative would be eternal damnation. The God of love, however, never rejects any of his creatures, but they, at least the rationally proficient of them, have the power to reject him. Until they repent, however, they exclude themselves quite deliberately from the greater fellowship of humanity which finds its fulfilment in the knowledge of God. Their conversion to the light is a matter of urgency both for their own well-being (so that they can begin to enjoy life to the full and no longer be imprisoned within the walls of material supports) and for the greater good of the community, who could gain so much from their unique contribution were they to proceed from selfish exclusion to loving participation.

In fact, to return to the question posed by Péguy above, none of us can come to God while any remain outside. A good analogy would be the heavenly banquet that forms so important a part of biblical allegory (Isa. 25.6–9, Matt. 8.11, Matt. 22.2–10). Could we, while sharing joyously in the festivity, bear to hear others outside begging for food? While the religious rigorist might actually rejoice at their misery as a proof of God's justice, those filled with the love of God, like the father of the Prodigal Son, would rush to open the doors and let them in to share God's bounty.

I thank you, Lord, for the privilege of my creation, the joy of being able to know you, and the promise of sharing in your very being. May I play my part in bringing closer the day when everyone will know you and work together for the coming of your kingdom upon earth.

That we may all
be One

❖❖❖❖❖❖❖❖❖❖❖❖❖❖❖❖ ❖❖❖❖❖❖❖❖❖❖❖❖❖❖❖❖❖❖❖❖❖❖❖❖❖❖❖❖❖❖

> God . . . whose will it is that all men should find salvation
> and come to know the truth.

1 Timothy 2.4

Our last meditation brought us to the brink of a view about
eternity called universalism, a belief that all humankind will
eventually be saved. It is a topic that arouses strong emotions for
and against; the judge in us all demands that a person pay the price
of his or her actions, while the more compassionate side,
remembering the obvious inequalities in one individual's life as
compared with another, looks for a deeper working out of justice
that sees the sinner's actions against the background of an
inscrutable presiding fortune. Jesus warns us categorically not to
judge and condemn other people lest we ourselves are similarly
treated (Matt. 7.1–2), while St Paul reminds us that we have all
alike sinned, and are deprived of the divine splendour, and all are
justified by God's free grace alone, through his act of liberation in
the person of Christ Jesus (Rom. 3.23–4).

One should add, however, that forbidden as we are to condemn
other people, we are told to judge actions by their effects, their
fruits (Matt. 7.15–20). We may be sure that God wants all his
creatures to attain salvation, to be perfectly healed of their
encumbrances, and to know the truth of his love. This love is the
essence of his creation of the universe: God loves everything he
has made, not only human but also animal, plant and mineral.
Dante movingly speaks, in the *Paradise* section of *The Divine
Comedy*, of the love that moves the sun and the other stars. Love
will never fail (1 Cor. 13.8), even if the beloved casts that love into
the mud. It is God's nature always to have mercy, and this mercy is
more than just a gracious clemency for a wrong that has been done.
It is such an ardent devotion that the sinful member will always be
held in the deepest concern even when its perversity appears to be
beyond healing.

122

Furthermore, as St Paul reminds us, God's love has been shown even more categorically in the healing work of his Son Jesus Christ. To believe in him as an act of faith is to be in his company, in the very presence of one who gave of himself profligately while he was on earth with us, so that we too might know something of the kingdom of heaven, as did the multitudes who experienced his healing touch while he was working with them. To accept the Lord Jesus is to find salvation, but this acceptance is something more than a verbal formula of assent. It is an opening of the whole personality in burning trust to the providence of God as witnessed in Jesus, so that his Spirit, the Holy Spirit, may pervade us, bringing new life to body and mind alike. It requires utter humility, honesty of perception, and an amended attitude to life that will reveal itself in service to all that lives.

The weakness of an unqualified universalism is that it bypasses the free will of the individual. It is therefore imperative that a person should remain in a hell of his or her own making until there is a genuine repentance that finds its expression in a humble confession and a heartfelt request for absolution. How long the recalcitrant person may reject God's overtures is beyond our reckoning, but I believe that eventually the hard shell cracks to reveal a palpitating soul longing for reconciliation and peace. The famous words from St Augustine's *Confessions*, 'Thou hast made us for thyself, and the heart of man is restless until it finds its rest in thee', seem to be the heart of the hope of universal salvation. Even the basest person has some awareness of God in the soul, clouded as it may be by destructive impulses that speak only of death. It is not unreasonable to hope that in the end the light will not be mastered by the darkness, but will instead illuminate it in its radiance (John 1.5).

Meanwhile God waits patiently to receive the penitent sinner back into the fold.

I thank you, Lord, for the privilege of my own special identity and the joy your presence in my soul gives me. May I so serve your will that I am able to bring many lost sheep into your fold so that, with one accord, they may bless your holy name and start to bring heaven nearer to the earth.

EIGHT

Creation and Resurrection

The Blessing of Life

❖❖❖

Bless the Lord, my soul,
and forget none of his benefits.

Psalm 103.2

It is a useful as well as an inspiring reflection at the end of the day to consider all the good things that have happened, all the happiness that one has experienced, all the valuable connections one has made as a prelude to the time that is to be. The scale of benefits gives one some indication of one's spiritual condition. To the unawakened person the good things will be material benefits, the happiness sensual pleasures of one type or another, and the valuable connections people of high degree in their various professions or social rank who can help one on in one's career. None of this is to be derided, but the transience of all purely material benefits is too obvious to be denied.

Thus Jesus tells the parable of a man whose land yielded heavy crops; he had so much surplus that he did not know what to do with it, and so he decided to replace his present storehouses with larger ones in which to deposit the crops. Then he could relax in the certainty of many years of plenty. But suddenly God called him, warning him that he would have to surrender his life that very night. Where would his riches get him now? This is how it is for a person who amasses private wealth but remains a pauper in God's sight (Luke 12.16–21). It is not the material benefits that are wrong, but rather the use of them as unfailing bastions of support, that God condemned.

Following on from this parable, it is evident that the benefits so vital to the unspiritual person will have to be taken away before a more mature grasp of God's bounty will be shown to him or her. 'Do not store up for yourselves treasure on earth, where it grows rusty and moth-eaten, and thieves break in to steal it. Store up treasure in heaven, where there is no moth and no rust to spoil it, no thieves to break in and steal. For where your treasure is, there will your heart be also' (Matt. 6.19–21). It is this treasure that should be the source of our unending songs of praise to God.

126

When, like Job, but hopefully not as radically, we have to surrender all the things that make life worth living — family relationships, possessions, reputation, and even our health — we are not entirely bereft, provided the house which is our life has been built on rock and not on sand (Matt. 7.24–7). It is our inner life, where high aspiration is founded on integrity and educated by compassion, that alone can withstand the adversities afflicting us day by day. In the words of H. F. Lyte's famous hymn, 'Change and decay in all around I see: O Thou who changest not, abide with me.' If our life has been one of unfailing service outwardly and prayer within, the jewels of our character will coruscate all the more brightly when we are enveloped in the darkness of material gloom and emotional turbulence.

When we know this inner domain, we are then worthy of receiving back our material benefits. Having by force of necessity as much as personal striving to return to the world of matter, we can use whatever riches are restored to us with detachment and for the benefit of others rather than for our own devices, remembering Jesus' words: 'Set your mind on God's kingdom and his justice before everything else, and all the rest will come to you as well' (Matt. 6.33). It is useful to remember St Teresa of Avila's bookmark:

Let nothing disturb thee;
Let nothing dismay thee;
All things pass:
God never changes.
Peace attains
All that it strives for.
He who has God
Finds he lacks nothing:
God alone suffices.

Thank you, Lord, that I have been privileged with the gift of life. May I so use it that my witness becomes a blessing to the many on the path who can scarcely distinguish between the darkness of illusion and the light of sanctity.

The Gift and
Responsibility of Life

❖❖❖❖❖❖❖❖❖❖❖❖❖❖❖❖❖❖❖❖ ❖❖❖❖❖❖❖❖❖❖❖❖❖❖❖❖❖❖❖❖❖❖❖❖

> The glory of God is a living man; and the life of man
> consists in beholding God.
>
> St Irenaeus, *Against Heresies*

It could well be asserted that humankind is the apogee of biological development on our planet, because we have the capacity to know God and enjoy his presence as part of our life. This knowledge has two components: an intellectual one that enables us to explore the universe and fathom the very process of creation (thus entering to some extent the mind of God), and an intuitive grasp of reality which finds its peak in a direct apprehension of the Godhead in mystical union. The impact of that mystical experience is so shattering in its radiance and power that no one who has known it remains the same, in so far as a new person is born out of the debris of old associations. The knowledge of God makes us more Christlike, as we play our part in the daily scene with a wisdom and love that we never previously knew.

And so we begin to know what living means — no longer a mere groping for existence in the bowels of the earth but now a joyful striding over its plains as every encounter shows us something of the divine splendour. Jesus said, 'I have come that men may have life, and may have it in all its fullness' (John 10.10). The same Gospel writer said of him that whoever received him and gave him their allegiance were given the right to become children of God (John 1.12). At last every faculty was fully awakened so that the spiritual realm was fully open to their gaze and consequently part of their existence.

In one of the most remarkable visions of Ezekiel, the prophet was carried by the Spirit of God to a plain full of bones. He was told to prophesy over them so that life might be restored to them and a mighty army arise (Ezek. 37.1–14). This was a symbolic prediction of the reanimation of the children of Israel; from their impotence

128

as captives in Babylon, they were to return to the Holy Land to rebuild the Holy City and its dominating Temple. More than even this, they were to grow into a mature understanding of their Jewish faith as a preliminary for their great contribution in providing the physical body of Christ himself. Their release from Babylonian captivity was an act of pure grace, an unmerited gift, of God, but they then had to put into action the promise bestowed on them. God gave them the potentiality for new life which they then had to realize.

There is indeed a type of life that is little more than an animal striving for pleasurable sensations, not necessarily bad in themselves but having no lasting effect either on the person or the world. There is also a life in the image of Christ that raises up the earth from death to immortality, from decay to resurrection. Such a life is a joy even when all the forces of destruction are ranged against it. But the saint is inviolate, because his or her vision is directed to God in rapt contemplation. As St Paul writes, 'Because for us there is no veil over the face, we all reflect as in a mirror the splendour of the Lord; thus we are transfigured into his likeness, from splendour to splendour; such is the influence of the Lord who is Spirit' (2 Cor. 3.18). This is the life of the fully realized person beholding God at all times, even when a crucifixion experience terminates the mortal span.

Of course, we little ones can hardly aspire to these spiritual heights, but if we remember to bring God into our lives, he will bring more life to us. We should start by the regular practice of contemplative prayer with its petitional, confessional and inter-cessory outpourings. If we really care for God and our fellow creatures, the divine presence will be with us ever more insistently, and life will flow through our bodies that will enlighten the world.

I thank you, Lord, for revealing to me the image of a truly alive person in the form of Jesus Christ. May I be so filled with your Spirit that the new fire flowing through me may be a source of renewal and healing to the world.

The Wonder and Glory
of Creation

❖❖❖❖❖❖❖❖❖❖❖❖❖❖❖❖❖❖❖❖ ❖❖❖❖❖❖❖❖❖❖❖❖❖❖❖❖❖❖❖❖❖❖❖❖❖❖❖❖❖❖❖❖❖❖

The heavens tell out the glory of God,
the vault of heaven reveals his handiwork.

Psalm 19.1

The beginning of this magnificent psalm rejoices in the perfection
of God's creative power; the whole universe is governed by laws as
perfect as the moral law entrusted to the people of Israel by the
supreme prophet Moses. It is an awe-inspiring thought that we can
rely on the constant flow of blessings from our Creator in the form
of heat, rain and the fecundity of the earth we inhabit, so that our
personal lives can continue in peace so long as we obey the moral
law that governs relationships with each other and also with the
soil from which we obtain our sustenance.

It may be objected at once that these universal laws not
infrequently seem to go adrift, so that climatic disasters hit large
areas of the world; but it should be remembered that there is a
place for chance in all cosmic phenomena: our earth is also
undergoing constant creation, and we have to face the fact of
terrestrial instability in some areas with a hazard of earthquakes,
volcanoes, floods and droughts. Nevertheless, these disasters are
the exception to the rule of cosmic order. We humans have been
put in a position of great importance in the scheme of our planet,
having been given dominion over the whole by virtue of our
enormous intellectual capacity. If our power is used adversely, not
only do we destroy each other, but we also wreak terrible havoc
upon our natural environment. It is not surprising that ecological
issues are playing an ever more dominant role in the thinking of
the rulers of the developed countries; those of the vast undeveloped
areas are often still fighting for survival and abusing their natural
resources accordingly.

How seldom have we the time or interest to gaze on and enjoy
the creatures around us! We are usually so engaged in our own

affairs that we take the natural scene for granted, and its beauty passes us by. Even if we do see, we seldom register; even if we hear, we seldom listen. Seldom do we think of nature except in the context of our own activities, so that it becomes a mere tool to use rather than a fellow creature to love. In the familiar lines of W. H. Davies' poem 'Leisure':

> What is this life if, full of care,
> We have no time to stand and stare?

We see how much we miss when our life is spent in moneymaking and mental speculation to the detriment of our part in the natural scene. God is not far from his creation even though he has given it the freedom to develop along its own lines. When we are imprisoned in a mental realm of material ambition, we are often blind and deaf to the world around us and to God who made it all.

It is one law that controls the universe and directs humans in right personal relationships. Its ramifications are infinite. Just as the heavens tell out God's glory, so do all his smaller creatures. So sustained are they by his providence that even a sparrow cannot fall to the ground except by his leave (Matt. 10.29).

> When thou makest darkness and it is night,
> all the beasts of the forest come forth;
> > the young lions roar for prey,
> > seeking their food from God.
> > When thou makest the sun rise, they slink away
> > > and go to rest in their lairs;
> > but man comes out to his work
> > > and to his labours until evening. (Ps. 104.20–23)

The Psalmist ends with the hope that the Lord's glory may stand for ever, and that he may rejoice in his works. He sings to the Lord as long as he lives, and is full of praise. May this be so for us also!

Thank you, Lord, for the privilege of an agile body and a fertile mind with which to serve you and make a grateful contribution to your glorious creation.

The Regeneration
of the World

❖❖❖❖❖❖❖❖❖❖❖❖❖❖❖❖❖❖❖❖❖ ❖❖❖❖❖❖❖❖❖❖❖❖❖❖❖❖❖❖❖❖❖❖❖❖

Behold! I am making all things new!

Revelation 21.5

This cry comes in a chapter of Revelation that begins, 'Then I saw a new heaven and a new earth, for the first heaven and the first earth had vanished, and there was no longer any sea.' A useful footnote in the Jerusalem Bible reminds us that the sea symbolizes evil because it was the home of the dragon (a wicked fallen angel or minor god, according to the legend of the ancient Jews and Babylonians); the sea will vanish as it did at the Exodus, but this time for ever, before the triumphal advance of the new Israel. The sea is also a symbol of the unconscious part of the mind in psychoanalytic theory. And yet the grumpy writer of the Book of Ecclesiastes solidly declares, 'What has happened will happen again, and what has been done will be done again, and there is nothing new under the sun' (Eccles. 1.9). He goes on to observe that even what appears to be new existed long before our time; the men of old are not remembered, and those who follow will not be remembered by those who follow them. We may argue that the scientific face of the earth is very different from the world of Ecclesiastes 2,300 years ago, but if we are honest we will have to concede that the hearts of people show remarkably little change from those who lived in ancient times. How easy it is to see elements of the adulterous David, the perfidious Ahab, the treacherous Judas Iscariot and the craven Peter in the depths of ourselves, to say nothing of those who wield great power in the world's councils!

Plus ça change, plus c'est la même chose (the more things change, the more they are the same), wrote Alphonse Karr in 1849 in *Les Guêpes*. It remains a cynical comment on human progress, but it is advisedly taken into account by all who have the welfare of their fellows at heart. Customs may change, but the human heart remains distressingly deceitful, desperately sick beyond all

132

fathoming (Jer. 17.9). The tragic decay of progressive social institutions is a sad commentary on the tendency we have to abuse general benefits for our own ends. In other words, the civilized behaviour of many people is simply a veneer which covers an animal concern for its own satisfaction at the cost of any finer feelings. When we return to our evening recollection of the day we have spent, we should not occlude our gaze from this part of our being.

While we live purely carnal lives we cannot advance spiritually, but when the Spirit of God descends on us and ignites the spirit within us where the Holy Spirit dwells as an unconscious presence, our sights are raised from mere survival to resurrection, from procreation to spiritual union with God and therefore with our fellows also. Fortunately the human spirit will never be content with earthly remedies for its strivings, because it has its home in eternity, the place of divine presence. This is closer to us than our own being, while at the same time transcending all categories of human thought and illuminating the noblest endeavour with a radiance that promises resurrection of all mortal elements to a new life in eternity.

It is this heaven that the writer of Revelation glimpsed. The world as we know it has its span no less certainly than any of its creatures; nothing of the universe is destined for immortality in its present state. 'What I mean, my brothers, is this: flesh and blood can never possess the kingdom of God, and the perishable cannot possess immortality' (1 Cor. 15.50). Whenever we are open to the Holy Spirit, whether in prayer or in our awareness of the present moment such that we can come spontaneously to the aid of a fellow creature in distress, a new life enfolds us. The mystic knows this particularly well at the moment of illumination, but we lesser people are included also when we give up something of ourselves for those around us. At that moment the unchanging face of reality that Ecclesiastes bemoans takes on the freshness of a newly born child, and we see it properly for the first time. But we must persist, lest the vision fades.

Give me the freshness of vision and the integrity of intent, Lord, to perform my day's work so excellently that both it and I may be a witness to your abiding creativity that works for the resurrection of the whole world.

A Promise
of Resurrection

❖❖

> He said not: 'Thou shalt not be tempested, thou shalt not be
> travailed, thou shalt not be afflicted'; but he said:
> 'Thou shalt not be overcome.'

Julian of Norwich, *Revelations of Divine Love*, ch. 68

As we come to the close of our series of night-time meditations it is
right that we should reach the peak of our endeavours. We are not
here simply to enjoy ourselves; we have also to make other people
enjoy us, to obtain real delight in our presence so that they also
may bring delight to the world.

> Man was made for Joy and Woe;
> And when this we rightly know,
> Thro' the World we safely go.
> Joy and woe are woven fine,
> A clothing for the soul divine.

So wrote William Blake in his *Auguries of Innocence*. We would
not appreciate the good things of life were it not for the
overshadowing evil that so often mars our delight. Once we have
come through a major surgical operation or a severe illness, we can
start to appreciate the wonder of health and also the precious gifts
we have been privileged to experience. These include not only
material possessions and human relationships, but also the integrity
of ourself and the faculties we have to appreciate the world and
travel into the vast mines of inner space.

Jeremiah's mission was, on the surface, a complete failure. His
compatriots would not heed his prophetic utterances, they detested
him to the point of planning his murder, and in the end the Holy
Land was ravaged by the Babylonians while he was forcibly carried
off to Egypt by a recalcitrant band of surviving Israelites, nearly all
of whom were to be destroyed by the Babylonians later on. But the

privilege of writing about God's new covenant with the Jews, in which the law would be set within them and written on their hearts, when a resurrected people would arise who knew their Creator directly and were spontaneously forgiven by him (Jer. 31.31–4), was of much greater importance than all the pain the prophet had to endure. The same scheme could be employed to trace the lives of all the great ones in the world's history, whether mystics, prophets, artists, musicians or scientists.

Without temptation, travail and affliction we would remain mere children; not the children who are to receive the kingdom of God but simply selfish, troublesome youngsters who act as if the whole world should revolve around them. Quite a number of highly successful men in public life are weaned from this childish selfishness only when retirement and bodily ailments cut them down to size, as they depend increasingly on the kindness of those who look after them. In other instances, domestic tragedies remind the outwardly prosperous where the true source of happiness lies.

Two sayings of Francis Bacon are worth reflection. 'It were better to have no opinion of God at all than such an opinion as is unworthy of him; for the one is unbelief, the other is contumely' (from his Essay 17, 'Of Superstition'). 'Prosperity is the blessing of the Old Testament, adversity is the blessing of the New' (from his Essay 5, 'Of Adversity'). Many images of God, including that of the savage potentate of the early Old Testament, are indeed contumely (a disgrace), but as the experience of humans grows, so a more amenable figure arises, as in Psalm 103 and the prophecy of Hosea. In Christ God shows himself as the Suffering Servant (prophesied in Isaiah 53) who takes on the full limitation of a man, in the end dying an agonizing death to the glee of most of the bystanders. He shows us something more than prosperity and happiness, that the end of the human, which we all have to face as death beckons us on, is resurrection to divine stature as we approach more fully the One who stands unceasingly alongside us.

I thank you, Lord, for the privilege of life, of humanity, and the promise of sharing in your very being. May the remainder of my days be so ordered that I draw ever closer to your incarnate Son in service and love, so that I may know you ever more intimately.